The Classical Tradition in **Anatolian Carpets**

The Classical Tradition in **Anatolian Carpets**

Walter B. Denny   with contributions by Sumru Belger Krody

THE TEXTILE MUSEUM
2320 S Street NW Washington DC 20008-4088

in association with

First published on the occasion of the exhibition
The Classical Tradition in Anatolian Carpets
September 13, 2002–February 16, 2003

The Textile Museum, 2320 S Street, NW, Washington, DC 20008-4088
www.textilemuseum.org

First published in 2002 by Scala Publishers Ltd
Gloucester Mansions
140a Shaftesbury Avenue
London WC2H 8HD
United Kingdom

Distributed outside The Textile Museum
in the booktrade by
Antique Collectors' Club Ltd
Market Street Industrial Park
Wappingers' Falls, NY 12590
United States of America

ISBN: 1 85759 283 2

All measurements are in centimeters followed by inches;
height precedes width

Edited by Slaney Begley
Designed by Andrew Shoolbred
Map by Technical Art Services
Produced by Scala Publishers Ltd
Printed and bound in Singapore by C.S. Graphics

Photographs are by: © The Textile Museum, Washington, photography
courtesy of Sotheby's New York, photographed by Ben Cohen, cat. nos. 1, 3,
4, 17, 18, 20, 25, 29, 34, 45, 47, 49; © The Textile Museum, Washington,
photographed by Franko Khoury, cat. nos. 2, 11, 32; ©The Textile Museum,
Washington, cat. no. 5; photography courtesy of The Cleveland Museum of
Art, Cleveland, cat. no. 6; © The Textile Museum, Washington, cat. no. 7;
photography courtesy of Marshall and Marilyn R. Wolf, cat. nos. 8, 16, 21,
24, 38, 42, 43, 50; photography courtesy of Sotheby's New York, photography by Ben Cohen, cat. nos. 9, 12, 19, 22, 23, 26, 27, 28, 31, 35, 36, 37,
39, 41, 46, 51, 52; photography courtesy of Jon M. and Deborah Anderson,
cat. nos. 10, 13, 14, 15, 30, 33, 40; © The Metropolitan Museum of Art, New
York, 1990, cat. no. 44; © The Jewish Museum, New York, photography
by John Parrell, cat. no. 48

Front/back cover: Carpet with ogival lattice design, probably south-central
Anatolia, 17th or 18th century, The Textile Museum R34.12.6, acquired by
George Hewitt Myers in 1913 (cat. no. 29)

Frontispiece: Detail of small-pattern Holbein carpet, central Anatolia,
probably 15th century, Marshall and Marilyn R. Wolf Collection (cat. no. 6)

Contents

The Textile Museum wishes to acknowledge with gratitude the generous financial support from the following individuals and institutions:

Jeremy and Hannelore Grantham
Sotheby's New York

The Textile Museum is grateful to the following private collectors and museums for their generous cooperation in lending to this exhibition:

Anonymous Collector, Pennsylvania
Jon M. and Deborah Anderson
A Massachusetts Collector
Marshall and Marilyn R. Wolf
The Jewish Museum, New York
The Metropolitan Museum of Art, New York

Acknowledgments

The book *The Classical Tradition in Anatolian Carpets*, as well as the exhibition at The Textile Museum, would not have been possible without the enthusiasm and support of many individuals and institutions.

We owe a debt of gratitude to directors, curators, and conservators who lent important carpets from their collections: Philippe de Montebello, Daniel Walker, Stefano Carboni, and Nobuko Kajitani at The Metropolitan Museum of Art, Joan Rosenbaum, Vivian B. Mann, and Susan L. Braunstein at The Jewish Museum. These loans have greatly enhanced the exhibition and have allowed us to focus on its theme. We are also very grateful to textile lovers who were extremely generous in allowing us access to their collections and providing information. The cooperation of William Ruprecht, Mary Jo Otsea, and Ben Cohen of Sotheby's New York, provided for photography, ably coordinated by Jennifer Heimbecker at The Textile Museum.

We would also like to extend our thanks to the Board of Trustees of The Textile Museum and to the staff of The Textile Museum for their encouragement and collegiality. Among the staff, we are especially indebted to Erin E. Roberts and Claudia L. Brittenham for their continuous support throughout the publication and exhibition production. We are also grateful to Ursula McCracken, Rachel Bucci, Theresa Esterlund, Mary Mallia, and Sonja Nielsen, who read and edited the entire text of this catalogue many times, and provided much needed advice and support. Richard Timpson, Doug Anderson, Frank Petty, Lynne Perdue, Rachel Shabica, Cynthia Hughes, and Anne Ennes went out of their way to accommodate our requests to make the exhibition more enjoyable for all our visitors. We are also indebted to Carol Bier, Cecilia Cash, Sandy Danielson, Crystal Sammons, Melissa Urda, and Sara Trautman-Yeğenoğlu for their continous support of this catalogue, exhibition, and related ancillary activities.

Walter B. Denny
Professor of Art History
University of Massachusetts

Sumru Belger Krody
Associate Curator
Eastern Hemisphere Collections
The Textile Museum

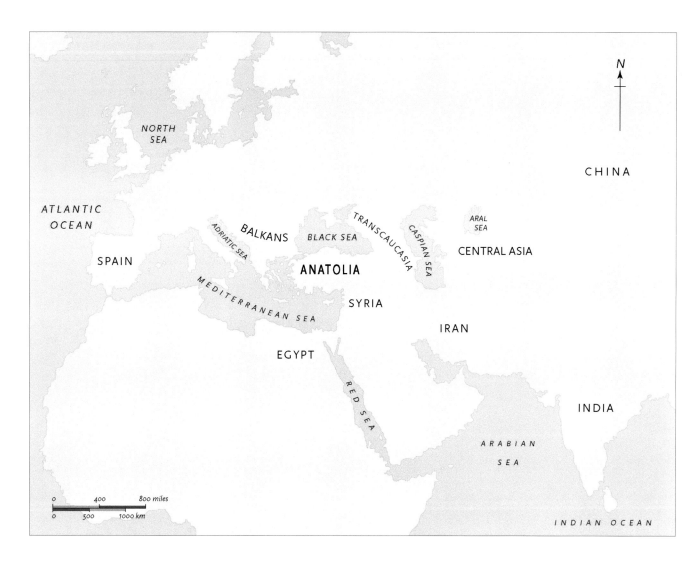

Anatolia and its Neighbors

Foreword

Anatolian carpets were not the only passion of George Hewitt Myers, the founder of The Textile Museum. His acquisitions also included Mamluk, Spanish, Caucasian, Safavid, Mughal, Central Asian, and Chinese examples. That is not to say Myers was random in his collecting. Rather, he was purposeful, with his acquisitions reflecting a focus on excellence. As a result, The Textile Museum is today the repository for many of the oldest and finest surviving carpets in the world (Bier 1996b). A collector and connoisseur, Myers was also concerned with utilizing his rugs and textiles to maximize their educational impact, through research, exhibition, and publication (Bier 1996a). It is thus with particular pleasure that we present this exhibition, its core drawn from Myers' collection, amplified and enriched by loans from private collectors and public museums.

Walter B. Denny, Professor of Art History at the University of Massachusetts, Amherst, is a man of energy and ideas. We are indebted to him for bringing together the concepts and intellectual structure for a study of the rich Anatolian carpet-weaving tradition from the fourteenth through the twentieth century. When I first became the Director of The Textile Museum in 1986, Walter was a Trustee, championing the staff's efforts to professionalize all aspects of the Museum's activities. It was with considerable pleasure that I recruited Walter to return in a different guise to curate this exhibition. Walter knows The Textile Museum collections well, in addition to being familiar with the major collections of classical carpets held in private hands the world over. He was the ideal scholar for this undertaking.

Jeremy Grantham and Hannelore Grantham inspired us to rededicate our efforts to Anatolian rugs. We are extremely grateful to them for their generous support that made this exhibition and catalogue possible.

The private lenders to this exhibition follow in the footsteps of Mr. Myers. Like him, they have a passion for carpets and carpet fragments, not only for their own enjoyment but also for the opportunity to instill in others an appreciation of fine craftsmanship and beauty. We are grateful to Sotheby's New York, who made their photographer and staff available to photograph carpets for the catalogue.

Ursula Eland McCracken
Director
The Textile Museum

Introduction

Oriental carpets have long been an integral part of religious and secular life, reflecting social status, commercial connections, wealth, and power; they have been expressions of refined taste and aesthetic sensitivity in many cultures for centuries. Whether used in mosques, in nomadic tents, or in urban homes, for prayer or daily living, Oriental carpets have served as essential home furnishings and items of luxury.

For more than 700 years, Oriental carpets were imported from the lands east of the Mediterranean Sea, and became a part of European and North American material culture and art. Europeans and Americans imported the idea, associated values and symbolic uses of carpets as well as the carpets themselves. Most Oriental carpets pictured in European paintings dating from the fifteenth to the eighteenth centuries were contemporary with those paintings. It was not until the late nineteenth century that collecting carpets, which exemplified the classical era of carpet manufacturing, became of interest. The first collections of these "classical" carpets were formed to provide a backdrop for collections of paintings, sculptures, and ceramics, which were displayed as works of "fine" art. At that time, Oriental carpets were seen as products of a craft tradition (Farnham 2001).

By the 1900s, the tide began to reverse itself and Oriental carpets, especially "classical" carpets, were deemed worthy of collecting by art enthusiasts such as James Ballard, Joseph V. McMullan, Robert Wood Bliss, and George Hewitt Myers. Scholars—Wilhelm von Bode and Ernst Kühnel among them—and the public started appreciating Oriental carpets as objects to study and as works of art. Oriental carpets were seen as products of creativity and artistic accomplishment that were influenced by cultures in which their makers lived.

Many of the carpets collected during this period enrich museum holdings today. Some collectors were very conscious of the significance of their collections and worked to place them in museums where they could reach a wide audience. George Hewitt Myers, founder of The Textile Museum, was such a collector. Myers started actively collecting Oriental carpets in 1909. His passion for carpets and other types of textiles, and his interest in educating others to appreciate this art form, led him to establish The Textile Museum as a public museum in 1925 (Bier 1996a, pp. 58–65 and Collins 1985, pp. 6–7). Carpets from the Myers' collection form the core of the presentation in this catalogue and related exhibition.

Myers wanted his collection to be available for study by scholars for the "edification and education of the public," and the enjoyment of everyone interested in Oriental carpets and other types of rare textiles (Lukens ms.). The beauty and variety of textile designs had a directness of appeal for him that other, what he termed "more self-conscious forms of art," did not possess. Myers considered weaving to be one of the most fundamental forms of human expression. He also noted that almost all cultures have felt the need to develop their own "textile-working techniques" (Lukens ms.). In 1931, he summarized his life as a

Detail of a Memling-pattern carpet, central Anatolia, probably 19th century (cat. no. 15)

collector for *The American Magazine of Art*. Speaking about himself in the third person, he wrote:

> The collection began with desultory purchases of "semi-antique" rugs, then gradually went into the earlier periods as the collector accidentally became aware of them, and became more able to spend the time and money to find and to buy them. He remembers distinctly when the first sight of a tattered old Ghiordes threw the spotlight of authenticity upon two or three of his own earlier purchases, which proved to be modern examples of this weave which had received an effective application of pumice-stone and "elbow grease!" It was evident that something was the matter, and his curiosity was aroused. This caused a moderate collecting of earlier pieces from Asia Minor, to be followed by the amazing discovery that "rugs" were made a long time ago in the Caucasus, Persia, India, China, and some other countries, as well as in Turkey and the Turcoman provinces whence the first purchases had come (Myers 1931, p. 335).

What preceded a piece and helped to make it what it was? This was the question that motivated and guided George Hewitt Myers to start collecting in the opening years of the twentieth century, and drove him to continue collecting throughout the first half of that century (Lukens ms.). For Mr. Myers, textiles from non-European cultures have had a coherent development; one that was recorded in their designs, colors, and structure. He believed that "politics, religion, economics, and geography, all had their influences on textile designs; conquest and defeat were recorded in their modifications and changes; the vitality or the decadence of people could not escape being recorded in this art form as well" (Lukens ms.). Myers started his collecting with Anatolian carpets and was actively acquiring them in the 1910s and 1920s. In the same 1931 article, he also described his collection of Anatolian carpets:

> From Asia Minor comes an adequate number of prayer rugs of all the well-known localities and of as early dates as are usually found. The Oushak-Holbein-Seben-Bergen-Transylvanian group are fairly well-represented and include a typical so-called Holbein in yellow on red ground, complete and nearly perfect, twenty one by twelve feet (Myers 1931, pp. 342–43).

By the time of his death at the age of 82 in 1957, Myers' collection had expanded to include nearly 500 rugs and over 3,500 of other types of textiles. Of these 500 rugs, 104 were Anatolian carpets. Since Mr. Myers' death, The Textile Museum has continued to strengthen the collections, and to share them with scholars and the public. In part due to collecting practices and the material available to the Western collectors at the time, Myers' interest in Anatolian carpets was focused on early Anatolian carpets. He rarely acquired any village pile or flat-woven rugs from Anatolia. The Textile Museum started turning its attention to these other weavings of Anatolia after the early 1960s. With the help of major donations in the 1970s and 1980s, the Museum broadened its holdings better to represent the full spectrum of Anatolian weaving.

The Classical Tradition in Anatolian Carpets represents The Textile Museum's commitment to Myers' collecting philosophy, to textile scholarship, and to the dissemination of knowledge to the public.

Design connections fascinated Mr. Myers. He was interested in how designs and motifs were adapted. In this catalogue and the related exhibition, Walter B. Denny expands on George Hewitt Myers' question of "what went *before* a certain piece to make it as it was." Prof. Denny proposes a unified theory of design origins for one of the oldest and richest carpet-weaving traditions. He asks many important questions: What were the major design sources that inspired the Anatolian carpet weavers? How can we recognize these sources in later Anatolian carpet-weaving traditions? How did a carpet with certain design and technical characteristics affect the carpet-weaving tradition? What was the impact of the techniques used in weaving on the designs produced? More specifically, did weaving techniques affect the adaptation or rejection of certain designs?

This catalogue, like the exhibition, is divided into nine sections. We start our survey with Anatolian carpets and their history. The history of pile carpets of Anatolia is complex because Anatolia has always been a rich blend of cultures, languages, and ethnicities. The second section discusses the relationship between design and weaving technique, and points out that while technique sometimes limits design making, at other times it enhances it. The section on Anatolia and its neighbors introduces us to the history and artistic environment in which these carpets were produced. It also prepares us for constructing a unified theory of carpet-design sources and for the presentation of major Anatolian carpet styles, which takes place in the following four sections. How these styles were formed and how they became a part of an Anatolian design vocabulary are the two questions Prof. Denny attempts to answer. The section on Anatolian prayer rugs is a case study of a specific group of Anatolian rugs. This group illustrates the endurance of specific designs and their transcription from one type of textile to another, from one culture to another, from one generation to another.

A weaver carries with her a design vocabulary developed by the generations that preceded her. Her personality, environment, and culture are also important elements that affect her work. A weaver combines the forces of tradition and individual personality to create objects that represent both her ancestral ties and her creativity. Thus, it is important to see both the continuity in design elements and the new perspectives that each generation brings to the process. This combination of continuity and change makes weaving a fascinating art to explore.

Sumru Belger Krody
Associate Curator
Eastern Hemisphere Collections
The Textile Museum

Essay

"What can be done with fewer assumptions is done in vain with more."
William of Occam (1285–1349)

Anatolian Carpets and History

In the history of art, perhaps no artistic medium, with the possible exceptions of brocaded silk textiles and Chinese ceramics, has managed to establish itself across major cultural boundaries to the degree exemplified by the knotted-pile carpet, conventionally termed the "Oriental carpet." Carpets woven in the Islamic world have been an essential part of the material culture of Europe and parts of the New World for centuries. They have acquired in their adopted lands a wealth of symbolism in part derived from that of their native culture and in part from new associations and uses. They have carried meanings of wealth, power, and identity, learning, taste, and sanctity. The art of knotted-pile carpets continues to flourish in the twenty-first century, against all odds and expectations.[1]

The knotted-pile carpets of Anatolia—today the Asiatic portion of the Republic of Turkey—constitute perhaps the oldest and richest carpet-weaving tradition, which survives in a significant number of examples today. Anatolian carpets form a highly diverse body of art, almost seven centuries old and immensely varied in technique, design, symbolism, and function.[2] These carpets were richly documented in European paintings from the fifteenth century onward, frequently mentioned in European inventories and other documents, and highly valued both as luxury goods and as works of art. Consequently, enterprising Europeans in locations as diverse as England and Spain, Poland and Sweden copied them.

For many, the terms "Anatolian carpet" and "Turkish carpet" are synonymous. Turkish invaders, migrating south and westward from inner Asia, reached what is today eastern Turkey in the late eleventh century and defeated the Byzantines at Malazgird in 1071. Then wave after wave of new arrivals from Central Asia migrated into Anatolia, where they settled and intermarried. Under their political rule, Islamic and Turkic culture gradually moved into a position of dominance, eventually replacing the indigenous Byzantine, Armenian, and other cultures of Anatolia. Until the cataclysm produced by nationalism, civil strife, and war between states in the early twentieth century, Anatolia remained a rich mix of cultures, languages, and ethnicities, a fact that both complicates and enriches the history of Anatolian carpets.

A hundred years ago, the oldest known Anatolian carpet examples were dated to the fifteenth century. The discovery early in the twentieth century of what were then thought to be thirteenth-century examples in Turkish mosques pushed the chronology of extant examples further back. These examples were later more confidently dated to the fourteenth century.[3] More recent carpet discoveries, however, have once again been attributed to the thirteenth century.[4] Before the thirteenth century, we have no concrete documentation for Anatolian carpet history, either in the form of actual carpets or reliable images of carpets. Byzantine and Armenian sources sometimes allude to production and trade of heavy textiles that may have been knotted-pile carpets, but of their designs, techniques, and artistic evolution we know virtually nothing.

Most surviving early Anatolian carpets show stylistic and technical similarities overwhelmingly associated by scholars with Islamic and Turkic artistic

Detail of a small Ushak medallion carpet, western Anatolia, late 18th century (cat. no. 35)

traditions, however diverse their ultimate origins may have been. Because the origins of Anatolian carpets are likely to remain shrouded in ambiguity, if not outright mystery, our narrative of their stylistic development must necessarily begin in the middle. As a sort of scholarly consolation, however, the abundance of examples that have survived since the Middle Ages presents us with a body of art that can be easily and coherently organized chronologically, and by design, although we still know relatively little about the provenance of its different groups.

If we take a broad view of the development of Anatolian carpets, using the full range of available evidence, we can see that a large proportion of carpets, dated with some confidence to the seventeenth, eighteenth, and nineteenth centuries, trace their common origins to a few small and easily defined groups. Most of these carpets were documented in fifteenth- and sixteenth-century European paintings. Some of these early carpets in turn can be related through stylistic evidence to a few even earlier carpets, as well as to developments in other artistic media in the thirteenth century, during the first great flowering of Turkish Islamic art in Anatolia under the rule of the Seljuks of Rum and their successors. Since we can document that these early carpets served as a continuing inspiration for Anatolian carpet-weaving art of subsequent centuries, we can characterize them as exemplars of a "classical" age of carpet style, a style that over the centuries has never gone out of fashion. Indeed, it has continued to the present day to instruct, inform, and inspire carpet weavers from the Aegean shores to the Transcaucasian lands, and from the Black Sea on Anatolia's northern coast to the shores of the White Sea (the Mediterranean) in the south.

In attempting to grapple with the origins of what we have chosen to call the classical tradition in Anatolian carpets, carpet scholars and collectors have identified two potential wellsprings that may have given birth to the designs of the fifteenth- and sixteenth-century sources of the tradition. For convenience, we may term these two conflicting points of view the advocacy of a style of place and the advocacy of a style of race. The former is the notion that the classical carpets arose from the pre-Turkish artistic traditions of Anatolia, including Helleno-Roman, Byzantine, and Armenian weaving. The latter is the idea that these early carpets reflect artistic traditions brought to Anatolia by the early twelfth-century Turkic invaders. These include what some view as the age-old nomadic artistic traditions of the Turkic tribes, as well as echoes of the Islamic visual culture acquired in Central Asia and Iran, as these Turkic tribes migrated westward. A number of individuals have argued for the persistence of a style of place. Celâl Esad Arseven and Herwig Barthels, for example, attempted to show by visual comparisons that there were pre-Islamic artistic survivals in early Anatolian carpets.[5] Various partisans of an enduring Armenian tradition have also found their way into print.[6] Neither of these points of view has met with much success among the broader spectrum of carpet scholars. Others, the present writer among them, have argued for the important but not exclusive role of the importation into Anatolia of artistic ideas by nomadic tribal Turkic peoples.[7] Perhaps inevitably, others, notably Murray Eiland and Michael David, argued against the whole idea of artistic originality among nomadic peoples.[8]

Today we are in a good position to reassess these arguments of the past century, and to look at the broader history of Anatolian carpets from a fresh perspective that lies between the poles of place and race. In order to do so, however, we have to date and define a chronology of those carpets that by common consensus constitute the earliest surviving Anatolian carpets. These can be divided into three broad groups. The first we may call the "painter" carpets, several hundred early carpets known for the sake of convenience by the names of European painters who preserved images of their designs and colors. These carpets are usually dated to the fifteenth, sixteenth, and seventeenth centuries, contemporary with the paintings. Holbein, Bellini, Crivelli, Lotto, Ghirlandaio, and Memling are among the European artists who inadvertently lent their names to early Anatolian weavings.[9] Carpets in the second group are usually termed "Konya" and "Beyshehir" carpets. The group consists of fewer than twenty carpets and fragments found early in the twentieth century, in mosques within those cities. Once dated to the thirteenth century, the carpets are now generally believed to date from the fourteenth.[10] The third group is made up of a few recently discovered carpets that conceivably can be dated to the thirteenth century. If so, they are the oldest surviving Turkish (and Islamic, for that matter) knotted-pile carpets, and hold the potential to help us toward a better understanding of the artistic evolution of "classical" Anatolian carpets and the importance of the classical style in subsequent centuries.[11]

Technique and Carpet Design

At first glance, the structural analyses of carpets that today form a standard part of catalogue entries may strike the casual reader as either superfluous or boring. In fact, there are many ways in which the technique used in the weaving of a carpet influences the artistic outcome. Frequently, the structure of a carpet can tell us a great deal about the carpet itself, something that we have attempted to illuminate in the text of the catalogue entries. Coloration and structure are sometimes a much more accurate indication of where a carpet was woven than motifs and designs. Knot type is, of course, important for grouping carpets geographically, as is the matter of spin and ply of yarns, especially in the case of the extremely rare use of S-spun wool. Ply of warp, weft, and pile can be of great interest as well. The ratio of knots per linear unit vertically and horizontally, which determines the pitch or angle of the diagonal used in the rug's artistic forms, is among the most important determinants of a carpet's design and visual impact.

Apart from structural analysis, questions of what materials were used are also important. The type of wool used might tell us many things; as scientific tests become more accurate, the analysis of fiber itself may help us to deal more accurately with questions of geographical origin and carpet age.[12] Dye analysis, using paper-chromatography technique, has already proven effective in determining where certain carpets were woven or where their dyestuffs originated.[13] Other scientific measures such as carbon-14 dating, have not yet proven to be of much use in dating carpets, but the technique is being refined and improved.

Of all of these matters, that of the degree of vertical elongation ("stretching") or compacting ("squashing") of a carpet's design is perhaps the most interesting, and has received the most attention in the entries in the present catalogue. The vertical/horizontal knot ratio is central to several of our most important arguments: for example, the thesis that the extremely rare and unusual "para-Mamluk carpets," with their almost perfect 1:1 knotting ratio, probably serve as a source for designs found in later Anatolian, Egyptian, and Syrian weaving.

The importance of the angle of the diagonal has been observed by scholars of the more recent Türkmen rugs from Central Asia, when examining a series of early rugs that were probably woven by the Salor tribe. The rugs are characterized by repeating rows of small geometric—in this case octagonal—medallions, which are thought to be some sort of tribal symbol, and are popularly termed as *gül* in the literature.[14] In rugs with this motif, the number of knots from the bottom to the top of the *gül* is almost always identical to the number of knots from the left side to the right side. And in the oldest Salor rugs, the measured distance from top to bottom of the *gül* is also equal to the distance from side-to-side. Over time, however, there appears to have been a progressive "squashing" of the Salor *güls*. Old salor rugs are recognized by their closely spaced warps, which give rise to a characteristic bi-level foundation. Later weavers may have perhaps tended to use more force in beating down each row of knots and wefts, and the warps came to be spaced further apart. In short, changes in the way carpets were woven led to fundamental changes in carpet design. Precisely the same process can be seen far to the west of Türkmenistan in Anatolia, in the case of the so-called small-pattern Holbein carpets to be discussed below. Here, only a very few early examples show a vertical:horizontal proportion of 1:1 in the basic *gül* motif, while later examples may reach a ratio of 1:1.5. The struggle to maintain an aesthetically desirable and iconographically suitable diagonal line appears to have preoccupied knotted-pile rug weavers in all Islamic lands for many centuries. On a simple level, it led to weavers using the expedient of offsetting each row of knots by one warp from the preceding row in order to achieve a steep diagonal in the design (cat. no. 1). On a far more complex level, it is probably the reason for the complicated patterns of inserting weft found in certain classical Persian carpets, such as the highly complex "vase-technique" carpets, with their mixture of wool, silk, and even cotton yarns.[15]

In the case of geometric patterns such as that used in catalogue number 1 and other Anatolian rugs, which consist of simple overall repeating geometric patterns on a small scale, it is logical to infer that the design may have been born from the technique itself, on the loom. Early experimentation by weavers within the strict discipline of the 1:1 knot ratio may have resulted in a good number of these simple geometric patterns, with their tendency to bi-color alternation and their prevalence of "hooked" motifs.[16] Undoubtedly some *gül* motifs came into being as symbols of various tribes, as the result of experimentation on the loom. It has been plausibly argued that other designs originated from non-carpet media—such as architectural decoration, silk textiles, or manuscript illumination—and were later adapted to carpet weaving.[17] In the case of such carpets, it appears that in general the earlier carpets, closer in time and in place to the original inception of a design, will be more likely to reflect the type of 1:1, vertical:horizontal, knot ratio common to many such designs. By contrast, later examples will exhibit not only the process of stylization—the gradual evolution (usually in the direction of greater simplicity) of motifs as one is copied from another in a long sequence over time—but also the process of "stretching" or "squashing" due to the modification of the weaving technique itself. It is very important to keep this in mind as we look at the almost perfect knot and design symmetry of the "para-Mamluk" carpets or the two very early *girih* rugs in the Vakıflar Museum in Istanbul, found in the Great Mosque of Divriği, and the lack of this symmetry in what we have defined as their many later artistic descendants.

In carpets of extreme fineness, the angle of the diagonal is almost irrelevant. Today weavers of ultra-fine carpets in Iran can duplicate almost any visual form, from paintings to photographs to paper currency, in carpets of incredibly fine weave, in the same way that a versatile ink-jet printer can produce an incredible number of dots of color per inch. In fact, the so-called "carpet design revolution" of the fifteenth century appears to have resulted from two different phenomena. The first was positive: the desire of carpet designers to utilize in their art a whole range of designs from other media, such as architectural decoration and arts of the book. The second was negative: the desire of carpet weavers and designers to rid themselves of the tyranny of the 1:1 knot ratio that made it so difficult to include curvilinear elements in their designs. The solution to both problems was to move to a greater knot density while at the same time attempt to preserve the 1:1 knot ratio. This meant that in addition to using finer weft and pile yarns, and packing the rug vertically, warps had to be much finer and closer together, thus often being forced into two levels on the loom. It led to the introduction of new materials (cotton and silk) and to new processes (machines for tighter, and more uniform, spinning and plying of yarns) in the making of carpets. And most important of all, it led to the deeper differentiation between weaver and designer. The entire complex business of designing carpets became the province both of professional court artists, working in court-subsidized workshops on royal commissions, and of designers attached to large for-profit commercial enterprises who looked to both domestic and foreign markets to sell their goods.

Anatolia and its Neighbors: History and Artistic Environment

It is the general nature of art to cross political, cultural, and geographical borders. The art of the knotted-pile carpet has been particularly successful in this regard. From the outset we need to acknowledge that Anatolian carpets did not exist historically in a vacuum. Documents and surviving carpets demonstrate the existence of early carpet weaving in Iran to the east, and in Syria and Egypt to the south. There is a complex interplay among these early traditions that has not yet been fully understood by carpet scholars. Shared patterns and motifs coexist with different preferences for dyes and coloration; shared symbolism and patterns of use coexist with marked variations in weaving technique. Dramatic political changes together with more subtle and evolutionary cultural changes add further complexity to the situation.

The early Turkic invaders of Anatolia in the eleventh and twelfth centuries appear to have brought with them, from Central Asia, a tradition of carpet weaving that was an essential part of the nomadic economy. Although few if any examples have survived from this time, the variety of rugs produced in the encampments of these early nomadic sheep-herders can be deduced from eighteenth- and nineteenth-century carpets woven by Türkmen tribes who stayed behind in what is today Türkmenistan in Central Asia. These rugs are mostly small and used as floor coverings, architectural decorations, festival decorations, and as containers for utilitarian objects in the *yurts* and black tents of the nomadic tribes. Türkmen knotted-pile rugs are often characterized by designs using rows of repeating small medallions, known as *güls*, which apparently serve as symbols denoting tribe, clan, or family groupings. *Güls* are easy to memorize and weave as patterns, and are suitable for decoration on small and large carpets alike. The nomadic Türkmen tradition of weaving carpets with stacked or staggered rows of repeating *gül* motifs undoubtedly moved into Anatolia along with the early invaders.[18]

At the beginning of the thirteenth century, the Turkish Seljuk culture of Anatolia, centered in cities such as Erzurum, Sivas, Kayseri, and Konya, was just beginning to enter its most important period of development. To the east, Seljuk Iran had been divided among provincial governors after the death of the last Great Seljuk sultan in 1157. To the south, the Ayyubid dynasty, founded by the legendary Saladin, had driven the Franks from Jerusalem and brought together Syria, Palestine, and Egypt under unified orthodox Islamic rule after the conquest of Egypt and its Shi'ite Fatimid dynasty in 1171. In the first half of the thirteenth century, Seljuk art blossomed throughout Anatolia. Fueled by a robust economy and the movement around Anatolia of artists of many different nationalities and cultures, working under lavish royal patronage,[19] the Seljuk synthesis led to remarkable and sophisticated accomplishments in architecture and the applied arts. By the middle of the thirteenth century, it had reached its climax in Konya, the Seljuk capital. There the mosaic tile decorations of the interior of the college, founded by the Grand Vezir Karatay (fig. 1), show us a beautiful and complex display of the so-called *girih* (literally "knotted") geometric style of interwoven strapwork, together with complex inscriptions using the angular form of Arabic script known as kufic. At the same time, a decorative border design directly inspired by kufic script but itself unreadable, often termed kufesque, also formed a common element in architectural decoration (fig. 2). Yet another form of decoration popular at this time in Anatolia was a curvilinear vegetal arabesque (fig. 3), incorporating a distinctive split-leaf form known in Iran as *islimi* and in Anatolia as *rumi*—Rum (literally "Rome," the land of the late Roman or Byzantine empire) being the Seljuk name for their new Anatolian homeland.

Fig.1 (facing page, top) Detail of dome with kufic inscriptions and *girih* arabesque decoration, Karatay Medrese, Konya, *c.* 1250
Photography by Walter B. Denny

Fig.2 (facing page, bottom) Detail of wall with calligraphic and plaited kufesque decoration, Karatay Medrese, Konya, *c.* 1250
Photography by Walter B. Denny

Fig.3 (above) Detail of tiled *mihrab* with *rumi* decoration, Sahib Ata Medrese, Konya, *c.* 1271
Photography by Walter B. Denny

From this artistic crucible were born the first great Seljuk court carpets, with designs apparently derived from Seljuk architectural decoration in tile, stonework, and carved wood. A fragmentary thirteenth-century carpet found in 1973 in the Great Mosque of Divriği, now in the Vakıflar Museum, Istanbul, shows us the style (fig. 4).[20] Hexagonal medallions of *girih* geometric style demonstrate a coherent pattern of white, interwoven strapwork, which forms complicated colored geometric stars and bars in the background. The complex and carefully planned kufesque border, also inspired by Seljuk architectural decoration, clearly recalls the beauty of Arabic calligraphy while avoiding spelling out holy writ whose use underfoot would have been inappropriate. Another carpet thought to be of the same early period, with a different weave structure and coloration, shows the same use of geometric forms, this time smaller ones repeated in rows (fig. 5).

It is probably from this thirteenth-century Anatolian tradition that the examples we most frequently associate with what is here called the classical tradition in Anatolian carpets—the largely geometric small-pattern and large-pattern Holbeins, Memlings, and others, with their interlaced *girih* design elements and early kufesque borders with distinct calligraphic finials—arose. There is also evidence that carpets with closely related designs might have been woven in neighboring lands by the fifteenth century.

Shortly before the middle of the thirteenth century, the Anatolian political situation changed dramatically. After they were defeated at Köse Dağ by the Mongols, the Seljuks were forced to pay huge sums in tribute to the Mongol Khan in Iran, and the power of the dynasty began to wane. As Anatolia fragmented into many small, separate states known as Beyliks, the scale of artistic enterprise, especially in architectural projects, diminished. However, the deeply embedded carpet-weaving traditions, which required far less capital and specialized labor than architecture and other media, continued to produce carpets throughout the fourteenth century. These carpets began to find new markets in Europe, where the nobility had developed new tastes for oriental goods in the aftermath of the Crusades. In addition, the emerging capitalist economy was developing the economic resources to afford such luxuries, together with the long-distance trade necessary to bring carpets, silks, spices, and technology to European markets. Mediterranean Sea trade, largely undertaken by Italians during this period, facilitated the flow of commerce from the Islamic lands of the east and south Mediterranean to the Christian realms to the west and north. European paintings and European inventories from this period begin to attest to the popularity of Islamic carpets in the West.[21]

While the Mongols permanently changed the political map of the Middle East, they were unable to conquer Syria and Egypt. There, the widow of the last Ayyubid monarch married her late husband's Turkish military commander in 1250; the rule of the Mamluks began and lasted until the early sixteenth century. The Turkic Mamluks, foreign rulers of the Arab populations in Syria and Egypt, were eager to participate in the European trade in carpets. By the fifteenth century, they had apparently set up government-sponsored factories to produce a distinctive type of carpet with designs based on a combination of Anatolian and Egyptian motifs, a limited palette of highly saturated colors, and wool yarns, which employ the distinctive counter-clockwise or S-spinning peculiar to Egypt.[22]

When the short-lived Mongol rule in Iran ended by the mid-fourteenth century, Iran fragmented into small principalities, which were briefly unified by the rise of

Timur (Tamerlane) in the late fourteenth century. Timurid culture blossomed most fully in the fifteenth century in its eastern capitals of Samarkand and Herat. The few surviving carpets attributed to the Timurid period demonstrate a very close design relationship with the early carpets of Anatolia. A significant number of depictions of carpets in early Timurid painting clearly show a design of stacked rows of small *girih* medallions like those of the "small-pattern Holbein" group.[23] By the late fifteenth century, Timurid power in turn waned and was replaced on Anatolia's eastern flank, in the part of northwestern Iran known as Azerbaijan, by the dynasty known as the Ak Koyunlu or White Sheep Türkmen, whose capital was the ancient city of Tabriz.[24]

We know from various documentary evidence of the fifteenth century that carpets were produced not only in Anatolia but also in the neighboring lands of Syria, Egypt, and western Iran. It appears that before the phenomenon known as the "carpet design revolution" began to dominate carpet production in the last part of the fifteenth century, the carpet traditions of all of these weaving centers

Fig.4 (above) Carpet with large *girih* octagons, central Anatolia, probably 13th century
Vakıflar Museum, Istanbul, A-217,

Fig.5 (left) Carpet with *girih* motifs, central or eastern Anatolia, probably 13th century
Vakıflar Museum, Istanbul, A-344

Fig.6 Detail of a carpet with medallion, vegetal, and *girih* strapwork star motifs, northwestern Persia, late 15th century
Museum of Fine Arts, Boston
William Francis Warden Fund, 65.595

may have shared elements of a common design vocabulary of geometric *girih* motifs, *rumi* design, and kufesque borders. The sharing of motifs such as the interlaced strapwork star among carpets of Syria, Egypt, and Anatolia, has long been recognized (cat. nos. 2–4). More recently, it has been hypothesized that a medallion carpet in the Museum of Fine Arts (MFA hereafter), Boston, which blends a field of rows of interlaced strapwork stars (fig. 6) in repeat with a multi-lobed medallion and floral vines, may document the impact of the "carpet design revolution" on carpets of northwestern Iran in the late fifteenth century.[25] Even more recently, the discovery of a silk-pile carpet with asymmetrical knotting that has been attributed by some to Timurid times (early fifteenth century or earlier), the chief motif of which is a remarkably coherent "large-pattern Holbein" octa-gon,[26] suggests that there may have been an almost universal *girih* carpet style based on geometric interlaced elements throughout the central Islamic lands in the fifteenth century.

In this context, we turn to the memoirs of the Venetian traveler and envoy Giosafat Barbaro. In 1478, in the course of extensive travels to Muscovy, Iran, and China, Barbaro arrived in Tabriz, where he hoped to develop Venetian-Ak Koyunlu diplomatic contacts with a view toward joint action against their com-mon enemy, the Ottoman Turks. He described his audience with the Ak Koyunlu ruler "Assambei" (Hasan Bey, better known as Uzun Hasan, r. 1453–1478) and the preparations for a great public festival in Tabriz. In the narrative of his travels, Barbaro mentions carpets several times, but one comment in particular is often cited in the carpet literature. Here it is, as translated into English in the sixteenth century:

> The daye folowing I prepaired to him [the king] into a great feelde wᵗhin the towne, wheare wheate had been sowen, the grasse whereof was mowed to make place for the tryomphe and the owners of the grounde satisfied for it. In this place were many pavilions pight [erected], and as sone as he pceauned [perceived] me he comaunded certin of his to go wᵗh me, and to shew me those pavilions, being in nombre about an cᵗh, [one hundred] of the which I pused [perused] xl [forty] of the fairest. They all had their chambres

whinfoothe [interior rooms], and the roofes all cutt of divers colo^rs, the grounde being covered wth the most beautiful carpetts, betwene which carpetts and those of CAIRO and Borse (in my judgement), there is as much difference as betweene the clothes made of Englishe woolles and those of Saint Mathewes.[27]

In the beautiful tent pavilions of appliqué work set up in a mowed field in preparation for a great festival, Barbaro observed the ground covered with "most beautiful" carpets. We must remember that Barbaro was a sophisticated and worldly Venetian, who was surely familiar with all kinds of Oriental carpets both because of his travels and because of the use of huge numbers of Oriental carpets in Venetian civic ceremonies. To understand his comparison between the carpets he saw in Tabriz and those of Cairo and Bursa, it is necessary to give some explanation of each of the centers he mentions. Cairo was famous for Mamluk carpets, while for Bursa we can read western Anatolian carpets, which Venetians would have purchased in Bursa incidental to their presence there to buy silk. To complete Barbaro's comparison, in the first half of the sixteenth century English wool was widely recognized as the very best in the world, while the cloth of "Saint Mathewes"—by which we may understand cloth of San Matteo—was apparently cheap and low-quality woolens sold at the San Matteo market near Santo Spirito in Florence.

It is important not to attach too much significance to Barbaro's statement. He was, after all, giving his opinion and was probably writing from memory long after the event. He might have been so moved by the splendor of the occasion as to venture into hyperbole. Barbaro, of course, tells us nothing about the design of these marvelous carpets. Still, it leaves us with the question of whether the carpets he saw in Tabriz were local products (as he seems to have assumed they were) and, if so, what a fifteenth-century Tabriz carpet might look like.

It is of course possible that Barbaro's "most beautiful carpetts" were similar to the above-mentioned early medallion carpet in the MFA, but there is no independent documentation of the date of such carpets, and the MFA carpet may have been woven somewhat later in the fifteenth century. Depictions in

Fig.7 Miniature painting depicting an Ak Koyunlu ruler, The Fatih Albums, late 15th century
Istanbul Topkapı Palace Museum, album H 2153, folio 91A

miniature paintings are of limited usefulness.[28] A miniature painting (fig. 7) that survives from the Ak Koyunlu court, now in the Topkapı Palace Library, shows what is believed to be the Ak Koyunlu ruler Ya'qub Bey (r. 1478–1490) with his entourage, sitting on a carpet that appears to have a repeating pattern of small knotted-outline medallions similar to the small-pattern Holbein carpets, with a white-on-red kufesque border with finials.[29] From this limited evidence we can logically infer that in the later part of the fifteenth century carpets with *girih* designs were still quite common at the Ak Koyunlu court, and were thought appropriate for inclusion in royal images. Could all carpets of the obviously distinctive type seen in Tabriz by Barbaro have perished? Or could it be that a few have indeed survived, but have not been recognized for what they are?

This brings us to the so-called "para-Mamluks" (figs. 8–9, cat. no. 4). This small group of surviving carpets and fragments is characterized by very precisely drawn designs based on *girih* geometry, a knot ratio very close to 1:1, kufesque borders of the "early" type with finials, a close affinity with various classical Anatolian rugs in motifs (large-pattern Holbein medallions, strapwork stars), and a color palette based on the familiar madder red. They show a very close

Fig.8 (right) Para-Mamluk carpet with large *girih* octagon and 2-1-2 layout, probably Tabriz, 15th century
Philadelphia Museum of Art, 55-65-2
The Joseph Lees Williams Memorial Collection

Fig.9 (facing page) Detail of a para-Mamluk carpet with 2-1-2 layout and *girih* strapwork star motifs, probably Tabriz, 15th century
Wher Collection, Switzerland

relationship with the symmetrically knotted carpet in the Vakıflar Museum, Istanbul (fig. 5). Remarkably unlike Anatolian carpets is the knot structure— asymmetrical knots open to the left.[30] The refinement and perfection of forms of the para-Mamluks arguably served not only as the source for motifs used in many later Anatolian carpets (cat. no. 2, where the strapwork star motifs were "squashed" vertically) and Syrian carpets (cat. no. 3, where the same motifs are "stretched" vertically) but also for the earliest Mamluk carpets of Egypt, typified by a magnificent example in the Museum für Angewandte Kunst, Vienna,[31] and, as noted, one of the earliest known northwest Persian large medallion carpets.[32] Two of the most important of the "para-Mamluk" group, in the Philadelphia Museum of Art[33] (fig. 8) and the Museum für Islamische Kunst, Berlin[34], have so-called "large-pattern Holbein" layouts. These show a particularly coherent and complex *girih* strapwork, arabesque, octagonal medallion as well as a very early variant of the kufesque border, again pointing to the role of this group as an early wellspring of some of the most important designs to be found in later Anatolian, Syrian, Egyptian, and Iranian carpets. Arguably para-Mamluk carpets served as the inspiration for the designs of the earliest Mamluk carpets of Egypt[35] and the strapwork star carpets probably woven in Syria (cat. no. 3), and they paralleled in development the more colorful large-pattern Holbein carpets of Anatolia. Given their fine weave, delicate and limited palette, and exquisitely planned designs, suggesting a court origin for the para-Mamluk carpets seems entirely reasonable; their color scheme is similar to that favored in Ottoman court carpets at the end of the sixteenth century. It is entirely possible that they may have been woven in the Ak Koyunlu realms, probably around Tabriz, where their designs, and their westward and southward diffusion over paths of trade in the fifteenth century, would have been accomplished with ease.

If the "para-Mamluk" carpets may have constituted eastern neighbors of the classical Anatolian carpets, carpets woven in Syria may have constituted a set of southern neighbors. While most scholars are comfortable with the idea of certain Mamluk carpets dating to the fifteenth century, there is little we can attribute to Syria before the late sixteenth century, when the carpets we call "chessboard" or "Damascus" carpets appear to have been produced (cat. no. 3). These commercial carpets, often woven in fairly large sizes, share certain decorative elements with their Anatolian neighbors to the north, but the technique and materials are quite different. Designers and weavers of Anatolian carpets of all kinds, including the commercial products of Ushak, rarely undertook the careful planning necessary to ensure a harmonious turning of the main border in the corners. By contrast, this trait is found in all "Damascus" carpets, whatever their field designs. While the geometric "chessboard" field design is most commonly to be found in those rugs assigned to Syria, they were also woven in a remarkable variety of curvilinear designs in different color schemes that would hardly seem to belong to the same weaving group. Notable examples are to be found in the Museum für Islamische Kunst, Berlin;[36] the Vakıflar Museum, Istanbul;[37] and in the recently discovered pair of fragmentary multiple-medallion carpets now in the Museum of Turkish and Islamic Art (TIEM hereafter), Istanbul.[38] Clearly, by the time that they were woven in the late sixteenth and seventeenth centuries, their designers were adapting many different kinds of designs and motifs to Syrian use, but, remarkably, all of the curvilinear designs in these Syrian carpets appear to have come from Iran. Why not the geometric designs as well?

Is it premature to suggest a sort of "unified-field theory" that links together the classical carpets of Anatolia with their neighbors, and to suggest a source for their designs in thirteenth-century Anatolia? Is it premature to assign the "para-Mamluks" to northwestern Iran, and to regard them as the wellspring for many Syrian and Egyptian carpet designs? True, the date of the two early Vakıflar Museum carpets is not yet fixed with absolute certainty, although they are generally regarded as among the earliest carpets with *girih* designs. The provenance of the "para-Mamluks" remains a matter for dispute and conjecture. There are even doubts in the minds of some that the "chessboard" carpets and others of their technique come from Syria, or that the "Mamluk" carpets come from Egypt. The hypotheses put forward here, however, have at least two virtues. First, they offer an explanation that accords well with almost all of the available evidence. Second, keeping William of Occam's axiom in mind, they appear to involve fewer assumptions than any other explanation.

Geometric Designs in Classical Anatolian Carpets

All of these questions of origins of motifs, and the role of technique, come to bear when we look at the various groups of carpets with predominately geometric designs, which are here defined as major sources of the "classical tradition" in Anatolian weaving. The oldest of these design types are probably the two kinds of carpets known as "Holbein" carpets, after their depiction in two famous paintings by Hans Holbein the Younger. *The French Ambassadors*, in the National Gallery, London, features a "large-pattern Holbein" carpet on a table, and the portrait of the Hanseatic merchant Georg Gisze in the Gemäldegalerie, Berlin, features a "small-pattern Holbein" carpet on a table. Holbein carpets of both types also appear in the works of Italian, as well as French, Flemish, Spanish, and British artists.

Any attempt to construct a unified theory of carpet-design origins before the earliest extant examples were woven, must start with the large-pattern Holbein carpets. What we have suggested as the earliest known example (fig. 4), now in Istanbul, shows a design in complex *girih* style, consisting of two large octagons with remarkably coherent strapwork designs, in which the implied interweaving of the strapwork is very easy to see. The intermediate stages of stylization are fairly readily apparent in other examples. A mid-fifteenth-century carpet in Berlin[39] shows elegance, balance, and coherence of the strapwork; by the time of the weaving of a well-known early seventeenth-century example in Istanbul (fig. 10), in which large medallions alternate with pairs of smaller ones,[40] ground-motif confusion has taken place. The interstices of the interlaced strapwork have become the scattered motifs, and the strapwork itself has all but disappeared, turning into a dark-blue ground. By the time The Textile Museum example (cat. no. 11) was woven in the late seventeenth century, the parentage of the carpet is still completely apparent, but there is almost no vestige of the original geometric interlace strapwork decoration. By contrast, a remarkable Anatolian version of the design that, on the basis of its border, probably dates to the eighteenth or nineteenth century (cat. no. 12), still clearly recalls the thirteenth-century prototype in many ways. It includes a very accurate rendering of the cornerpieces, which suggests it was copied directly from a fifteenth- or sixteenth-century carpet rather than forming a part of a long chain of progressive stylization.

Fig.10 2-1-2 Large-pattern Holbein carpet, central Anatolia, 17th century
Istanbul Museum of Turkish and Islamic Art, Inv. No.468

The compelling fascination that the large-pattern Holbein design and layout had for the weavers of later centuries is recalled in numerous variants. For example, the so-called "2-1-2" examples (where pairs of small medallions alternate with a single large one) have been quite popular since the fifteenth century,[41] not only in Anatolia but probably in Tabriz as well (figs. 8–9). The 2-1-2 layout was so popular in the Middle East that it reached as far as Egypt, where the most celebrated of all Mamluk carpets—the silk-pile example now in Vienna—incorporated four small 2-1-2 layouts in its four corners.[42] By the nineteenth century, the large central octagon served as a major design inspiration for everything from Kazak rugs of southern Transcaucasia to small Anatolian cushion covers (cat. no. 13).

The early small-pattern Holbein carpets of Anatolia (cat. nos. 5–7) share many of the techniques, coloration, and secondary motifs of the large-pattern Holbein carpets, including the use of *girih* geometry, kufesque borders of both the "calligraphic" and "plaited" types, and certain motifs such as the *ashyk* or "knucklebone" border (cat. no. 5). Sometimes the two design types are actually combined in the same carpet; in a number of arguably early large-pattern Holbeins of the "2-1-2" type, the small-pattern Holbein *gül* is used as the secondary motif.[43] The small-pattern Holbein carpets also share one basic design feature in common with nomadic Türkmen weaving—an easily learned and easily inherited design of small, repeating, centralized forms, arranged in orderly stacked rows. Indeed, the appearance of the characteristic small-pattern Holbein "knotted *gül*" in a number of early Central Asian Türkmen carpets, largely attributable to the Salor tribe, constitutes one of the most important links between the Anatolian and Central Asian traditions.[44] Like the large-pattern Holbein carpets, the small-pattern Holbeins have a long legacy in Anatolian weaving that persists until our day (cat. nos. 8–9).

The characteristic motif known as the Memling *gül* (cat. nos. 14–15), which is easy to weave and striking as a major carpet motif, is perhaps the most popular of all of the classical carpet motifs to have survived in Anatolian weaving. The motif has been given its name from a depiction of a very small carpet, possibly a flat-woven carpet, in a still-life painting by the Flemish painter Hans Memling, now in the Thyssen-Bornemisza collection in Madrid.[45] The motif differs from the small-pattern Holbein *gül* in one crucial respect: there is no implication of three-dimensional interlacing or strapwork. Rather, the Memling *gül* is two-dimensional and almost certainly derives from the medium of weaving itself.

We may suppose that among classical Anatolian carpets, the Memling carpets are the most likely to have descended from nomadic prototypes without the intervention of ideas from other media. The simplicity of the Memling *gül* and its widespread diffusion among nomadic weaving traditions—in Central Asia (where it appears in Yomut and Tekke Türkmen weaving),[46] Transcaucasia (where it appears in the carpets of the Mughan steppe), Iran (in Shah Sevan and southern Persian carpets),[47] and Anatolia—also attest to the probable nomadic origins of the form. Since the Memling *gül* is so easy to weave and has no spatial ambiguities, it is the least likely of all classical Anatolian carpet forms to undergo the mutation process inherent in stylization as the form is passed by mother to daughter through many generations. For this reason, there is no readily apparent evolution of basic forms that assists us in dating such carpets. The two white-ground examples thought by consensus to be early rugs, in the Museum of Applied Arts, Budapest, and the Mevlana Museum, Konya,[48] differ very little in most aspects from more recent weavings.

Fig.11 Tile with *rumi* quatrefoil design and four lotuses, Sünnet Odası, Topkapı Palace, Istanbul, early 16th century
Photography by Walter B. Denny

Perhaps the most complex and enigmatic of the early classical designs found in Anatolian carpets are those of the "Ghirlandaio" group, whose eponym is found in a painting of the Madonna and Child by the fifteenth-century Florentine painter Domenico Ghirlandaio, now in the Uffizi Gallery, Florence.[49] The characteristic diamond-shaped Ghirlandaio medallion represents a syntactical rearrangement of motifs clearly visible in what we have suggested is a thirteenth-century carpet, the two-medallion large-pattern Holbein in the Vakıflar Museum, Istanbul (fig. 4). Belkis Balpınar first suggested in 1984[50] that the cornerpieces of the Vakıflar carpet were in fact representations of architectural forms: the *muqarnas* squinches found in Seljuk and Ottoman architecture, which make an architectural transition between a square building and an octagonal dome. Whatever their origin, these cornerpiece motifs were, through a weaver's originality, subsequently changed in orientation and arranged around the four cardinal points of a central octagon to produce the "Ghirlandaio" medallion.

The rarest of the "classical" Anatolian carpet types discussed here, not represented in the present exhibition, is the so-called "Crivelli" carpet type, whose eponym is a painting of the Annunciation in the National Gallery, London, by the northern Italian painter Carlo Crivelli.[51] There is only one fragmentary pile example thought to come from the classical age—in the Museum of Applied Arts, Budapest—and a relatively small number of descendants, among which one, a Transcaucasian sumak in the same museum, is of a much later date.[52]

Another classical type with many later descendants, represented in this exhibition by a single example that occurs in hybrid form with a "Ghirlandaio" central medallion, is the so-called Bellini carpet design, which displays a keyhole-like motif (cat. no. 19). This motif has been variously explained as a stylized version of a form that in Chinese art symbolizes a mountain[53] or as a depiction of a reflecting pool or fountain. The painting by Giovanni Bellini from which the name is derived is probably his 1507 portrait of the Venetian Doge Loredan, and four of his advisors, now in Berlin.[54]

As we have already seen, the secondary motif in small-pattern Holbein carpets is a quatrefoil composed of pairs of split leaves known as *rumi* forms (fig. 3). The same motif, ranging in forms from highly complex (cat. no. 20) to extremely simple (cat. no. 21), appears over the centuries in many different kinds of Anatolian carpets. Of all of the classical forms, the quatrefoil and its sub-parts, which consist of two split-leaf *rumi* forms embracing a lotus flower (fig. 11), are the most likely to have originated in non-carpet media. Found in all of the major Islamic carpet-weaving traditions from the fifteenth century onward, the quatrefoil is both ubiquitous and ambiguous, for its symbolic meaning—if indeed there is any—is today unknown. From its original use as a repeating pattern, the motif was later used as an independent medallion (cat. nos. 22–23), in which form it appears in countless descendants in a variety of sizes and genres.[55]

Judging from surviving examples, among the most popular of all of the classical Anatolian carpet designs is the yellow geometric *rumi* lattice on a red ground. Carpets with this design are called "Lotto carpets" from their appearance in a well-known altarpiece by the sixteenth-century northern Italian painter Lorenzo Lotto.[56] The earliest examples of Lotto carpets use what we have called the "calligraphic" kufesque border, with clearly denoted "letter finials" recalling kufic script. Later examples such as those in this exhibition, probably from the late sixteenth or early seventeenth century, show a wide variety of borders based on repeating multi-lobed cartouches (cat. nos. 24–25). In discussing Lotto carpets, Charles Grant Ellis grouped them according to three variants of the basic design, which he termed the "Anatolian," "kilim," and "ornamented" styles.[57] Most of the early Lotto carpets were woven in fairly large sizes, but as the pattern gained in popularity in later centuries, large numbers were woven in the smaller *sajjadah* or prayer rug size, of which an unusual dark-red ground carpet (cat. no. 26) is a good example. These smaller versions appear frequently in European paintings from many countries, and significant numbers have survived in the museums and churches of central Europe such as the celebrated Black Church in what is today Braşov (Brassó, Kronstadt), Romania.[58]

The "painter" carpets—Holbeins, Lottos, Bellinis, Ghirlandaios, Memlings, and Crivellis—all share the fundamental characteristics of highly geometrized designs that either have geometric prototypes or were adapted to the carpet medium from curvilinear prototypes. Clearly both artistic processes were taking place from at least the fifteenth century and probably much earlier. Carpets with the quatrefoil motif present an unusual problem in that although they appear in highly geometric form in the earliest of the small-pattern Holbeins, their *rumi* motifs are quintessentially curvilinear in origin. Architectural decoration would appear to be the most logical "outside" source for many of the motifs in these carpets. Only the "Memling" group would appear to show a design whose origins are probably rooted in the carpet medium itself.

Carpet Designs from the World of Silk Textiles

Another major theme in the history of Anatolian weaving is the interplay between two related but highly distinct art forms: patterned, woven, luxury textiles (often woven of silk) and knotted-pile carpets (almost always woven of wool).[59] As early as the fourteenth century, in what until quite recently was characterized as the earliest surviving group of Islamic carpets, we see, in a somewhat crudely conceived and highly geometric carpet discovered in the Great Mosque of Konya, a design that has been demonstrated to be a very literal adaptation of a curvilinear repeating pattern of lotus plants with trailing stems, taken from a fourteenth-century Chinese silk-damask textile.[60]

In general, the fineness of silk weaving on the complex loom known as a drawloom means that the rug weaver's problems with the angle of the diagonal are irrelevant, and designs of incredible complexity and fineness can be woven without undue difficulty.[61] After the Mongol conquests of the mid-thirteenth century, the opening up of commerce between western Asia and China meant that a flood of Chinese luxury goods, among them brocaded silk textiles and porcelain, began to move westward. At the same time, the impact of Chinese art on the arts of the Islamic world can be clearly seen. Once the carpet weavers of Anatolia started reproducing the patterns of Chinese and other textiles, the tradition continued for many centuries. In the exhibition, we have shown a number of carpets where the impact of silk weaving is clearly apparent on several different levels.

One major impact of silk weaving on carpets, not apparent in the early Chinese-inspired example from Konya, is that of layout. Silk weavers in fifteenth-century Egypt and Iran were fond of a layout called an ogival lattice, in which a continuous lattice of *rumi* forms helped to define staggered rows of compartments with rounded sides and pointed ends. By the late fifteenth century, this kind of layout had also affected Ottoman silk weaving. Fragmentary examples of silk textiles evidently woven in Turkey from this time have survived, and are incorporated in the doublures or inner bindings of a number of dated or datable books from the Ottoman court (fig. 12).[62] By the sixteenth century, the ogival layout was one of the most popular in use in the Ottoman velvet-weaving center of Bursa. It was also found in vast numbers of brocaded silks evidently woven in the neighborhood of Istanbul, and it continued to be popular well into the seventeenth century and beyond.[63] If we look at Anatolian carpets with the ogival lattice design, we can easily distinguish between those using an "early" prototype, where the lattice itself is composed of split-leaf *rumi* forms, and a "later" prototype, where the lattice is more likely to be a ribbon-like band, and the contents of each compartment include the post-1550 Ottoman design repertoire of tulips, carnations, hyacinths, and roses.[64] Four carpets from the exhibition are among those likely to be of the "early" group. Catalogue number 27, probably the oldest, is a fragment with a pattern of blue *rumi* lattice on an unusual pale-brown ground. The center of each compartment displays a number of blossoms on a delicate vine arabesque, with a large butterfly-like lotus blossom in the center, a motif we have already seen in varying geometric and non-geometric incarnations in early small-pattern Holbein (cat. nos. 6–7), quatrefoil (cat. no. 20), and Lotto (cat. nos. 24–26) carpets, and in architectural tile decoration as well (fig. 11). The prototype for catalogue number 27 is very likely to have been a fifteenth-century textile; whether it was an Ottoman, Mamluk, or even possibly a Timurid silk textile, is still a matter for speculation.

A much later carpet, catalogue number 28, likewise clearly shows the split-leaf *rumi* forms in its ogival lattice, but the simplified geometric design brought about by the "tyranny of the diagonal" leaves the prototype much more in doubt. Also inspired by an ogival textile is a carpet from The Textile Museum (cat. no. 29), with a blue-green ground, where the red lattice encloses three highly geometric floral forms in each compartment. In this carpet, the still-visible intimations of fluid, curvilinear design from the silk-textile prototype make an intriguing contrast with the archaic angularity of the kufesque border. Finally, a fourth rug—this one a small *yastık* or cushion cover from western Anatolia that was probably woven almost two centuries later (cat. no. 30)—uses almost exactly the same design. Turkish silk velvet *yastıks,* woven in Bursa and later also in Üsküdar over a period of several centuries, often show evidence of a very similar "excerpting" of quotations from much larger repeating patterns.

The velvet cushion covers from Bursa looms evidently enjoyed great popularity in Anatolia over the centuries and they were copied or adapted repeatedly in pile format by village weavers. One example in the exhibition, shown side-by-side with its velvet prototype (cat. nos. 32–33), demonstrates the skill with which an Anatolian village weaver was able to breathe new life and color into a *yastık* design.

Finally, while it must be noted that, in general, Anatolian carpet weavers appear to have preferred woven, silk-textile designs as inspiration for many of their carpet designs, there are also many examples of embroidered textiles having influenced the Anatolian weavers. This important aspect of Anatolian carpet weaving is represented in the exhibition by a small pile *yastık,* probably woven a little over 100 years ago (cat. no. 31). Here the weaver has adapted to the knotted-pile carpet technique a fairly well-known embroidery pattern, which in the original was created in needlework of colored silk threads on a piece of cotton

or linen foundation fabric. It is one more testament to the variety and imagination found in the artistry of Anatolian village weavers, as they reacted creatively to the art of other times and other media.

Fig.12 Silk fabric in the doublure of a book with a *rumi* design, probably Istanbul, 3rd quarter of 15th century Istanbul Topkapı Palace Museum, A 3236

The "Design Revolution," Ushak Production, and its Imitators

Up to this point, we have presented the roots of what we have characterized as the classical tradition in Anatolian carpets either as stemming from very old traditions of geometric design, whose origins are veiled in the murkiness of textile history, or evolving as a response to designs in another textile medium, that of brocaded silk textiles. Indeed, if we survey the later centuries of Anatolian weaving, a very large proportion of the extant carpets belong to these two groups. However, there are two other major early sources for motifs and designs in the later Anatolian tradition that can, by right, take their places alongside the "painter carpets" and the "textile carpets" as fundamental pillars of the classical tradition in Anatolian carpet weaving. These are carpets based on designs created by professional artists employed by the Ottoman imperial court in Istanbul, and the commercial carpets of Ushak.

Ushak (Turkish: *Uşak*) is today a moderately sized market town in west-central Anatolia. Little remains to suggest that in the fifteenth century it may have produced carpets for the Ottoman court in Istanbul and that, from the sixteenth century onward, one of the largest productions of commercial carpets in history was centered in this town and in its surrounding villages. Ushak carpets survive in prodigious numbers; three decades ago, large seventeenth-century Ushak carpets in the most familiar format—the ogival medallion with pendants—

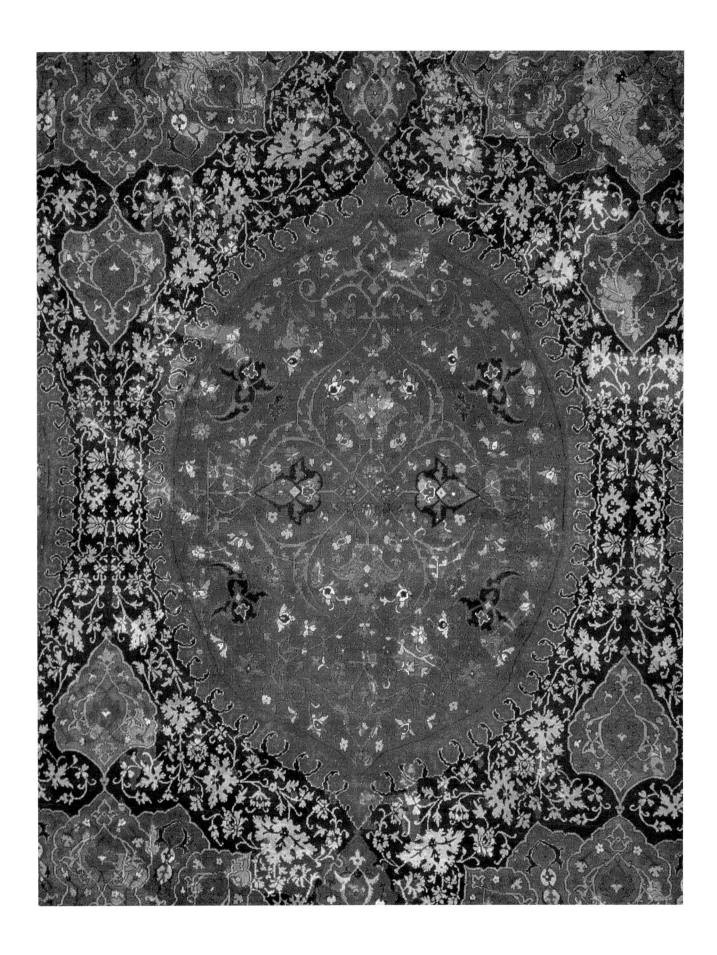

sometimes sold at auction for far lower prices than twentieth-century commercial Persian carpets of similar or smaller size. The carpets attracted very little attention from carpet scholars, but this situation changed with the publication of a two-part article by the British scholar Julian Raby in 1986.[65]

In the article, and later in an important book[66], Raby argued that the designs of perhaps the most famous and numerous of Ushak carpets, called the medallion Ushak carpets (fig. 13), were closely related to the overall development of Ottoman Turkish art in the fifteenth century. He suggested that the earliest Ushak medallion carpets, which do not begin to appear in European paintings until the middle of the sixteenth century, were products of the late fifteenth century, not of the sixteenth century. The publication by Alberto Boralevi in 1987 of the "Castellani-Stroganoff" Ushak medallion carpet, an example with a "hybrid" border of kufesque forms combined with more traditional Ushak border motifs,[67] gave further strength to the notion that the Ushak weaving tradition might be a good deal older than previously thought. Recently, Carlo Suriano's article on early Ushak carpets examined the entire early group in more detail.[68] In addition to reviving interest in Ushak carpets from a scholarly point of view, these publications also raised another, even more intriguing question of where and when the so-called "carpet design revolution" may have taken place.

To understand the importance of this question, we must first look at the original hypothesis of a "design revolution" put forward by Kurt Erdmann in the 1950s.[69] In looking at the history of carpet design, Erdmann noted that those carpets thought in his day to be the earliest surviving examples, attributed to before 1500—including many of the "painter carpets" and their predecessors, the "Konya" carpets—had, without exception, geometric designs. He also noted that the majority of the greatest masterpieces, thought to have been woven in the sixteenth century and later, had elaborate curvilinear designs and often a much finer weave. In surveying the evidence of representations of large carpet-like textiles available in miniature painting, Erdmann then decided that the "revolution" in carpet design must have occurred in the late fifteenth century and that the place of this revolution was probably the Timurid court of Herat, today in Afghanistan, but in the fifteenth century both politically and culturally a part of Persia.[70]

Erdmann's evidence was largely taken from miniature paintings, for then as now Erdmann and other carpet scholars were unable to identify any surviving carpets with curvilinear designs actually thought to have been woven in Herat around the time of the "revolution." Herein, of course, lies one weakness of Erdmann's argument, and indeed of any scholarly argument about carpet history before the weaving of the earliest surviving examples. Another weakness beyond the lack of "ancestors," however, is the lack of "descendants." There is the odd resemblance between medallion carpets in miniature paintings and actual carpets.[71] However, most of the representations of large, colorful textiles in the paintings of Behzad and other artists who worked at the Timurid court in Herat in the late fifteenth century—many of them represented as canopies hung from poles—bear only the most precarious visual resemblance to surviving carpets of Persia.

There is no doubt that Erdmann's "revolution" actually occurred. At some time and place during the fifteenth century, carpet designers did start to create a brand new kind of design, which in the sixteenth century led to some of the greatest masterpieces in the history of this art form—what the late Richard Ettinghausen once referred to as the "real heavyweights" of carpet art. But the

Fig.13 Detail of a medallion Ushak carpet, early 16th century
Kuwait National Museum, al-Sabah Collection

weaknesses in the Herat painting hypothesis might lead us to ask the simple questions: "If not Herat, then where? And how?" The relationship between arts of the book—art created in a very small scale on pieces of paper or tooled leather, which served as the folios and bindings of lavishly decorated books made for Islamic rulers—and other art forms in Islamic art, is very well-demonstrated. There is no question that in the sixteenth century and later, designers trained in the arts of illumination and miniature painting influenced or even actually created carpet designs in the Safavid (Iran), Ottoman (Turkey), and Mughal (India) Empires. What Julian Raby pointed out in his 1986 paper[72] and in the following decade in a much more broadly documented fashion,[73] is that many surviving Ushak carpets clearly reflect a very specific style, present in bookbinding and illumination of late fifteenth-century Ottoman Istanbul, not of the late fifteenth-century Timurid Herat. Beyond any doubt, the secondary "oak leaf" ornament of the early Ushak medallion carpets reflects the style associated with the Istanbul court designer and illuminator known as Baba Nakkaş. The parallels between the medallions themselves and early fifteenth-century Ottoman tile decoration from Bursa have also been pointed out.[74] Therefore it is entirely reasonable to assume that some of the earliest of these Ushak medallion carpets may have been woven at least as early as the last quarter of the fifteenth century, quite possibly to the order of the Ottoman court in Istanbul for use in the royal palace. In the sixteenth century, when other tastes began to prevail in Istanbul, such carpets began to be exported to Europe in significant quantities, and the taste for them continued in countries such as the Netherlands well into the seventeenth century.[75] While this hypothesis does not rule out the possibility that the "design revolution" may have occurred simultaneously in several places in the fifteenth century, it does shift our focus of attention westward, specifically to Istanbul, Anatolia, and to the Türkmen court in Tabriz.

Lost in all of the scholarly excitement over the medallion Ushak carpets were the so-called "star" Ushaks, the most popular and numerous type of Ushak carpet after the medallion type, represented in the exhibition by a carpet from The Textile Museum (cat. no. 34). Raby had in fact pointed out a very close relationship between the standard "star" Ushak design and two Ottoman bookbindings in manuscripts dedicated to Sultan Mehmed II (r. 1451–1481).[76] But when we try to establish a specific relationship between Ushak carpets and the Ottoman decorative style, it is useful to remember that the Ottoman decorative style in the late fifteenth century was in fact one manifestation of a broader "international style" that developed along a Tabriz-Istanbul axis. The new artistic developments affecting both Anatolia and Iran during the period were likely to crop up not only in Ottoman Istanbul but also in Türkmen Tabriz. The thriving commerce in raw silk between Tabriz in the east and Ottoman Bursa in the west bound the two regimes together in many other ways as well, and Anatolia (and thus Ushak) was positioned between the two poles of this axis.

Raby urged us not to see the development of Ushak carpets as a carpet-to-carpet transfer of artistic ideas but rather as a consequence of "a general change in Ottoman decorative arts."[77] It might be preferable to consider this instead as "a general change in Ottoman/Türkmen decorative arts." We might then find it easier to recognize that "star" Ushak carpets, in addition to having a resemblance to certain examples of Ottoman court bookbinding, also demonstrate a clear relationship with another art form that is far closer to them in both scale and function: architectural tile decoration. Tile decoration covers vertical architectural surfaces (walls). Carpets cover horizontal architectural surfaces (floors). In concept, the designs of most Ushak carpets repeat endlessly in four directions, rather than accommodate to the dimensions of the carpet. Thus, the infinite nature of their designs and their large size are closely akin to the decorated, tiled surfaces found in late fifteenth-century Islamic architecture. Such tiled architecture is not found in the Ottoman domains where, by the second half of the fifteenth century, large-scale tile decoration seems to have gone out of fashion. In nearby Tabriz, however, it remained popular. The greatest surviving monument of Türkmen architecture, the Masjid-i Kabud or "Blue Mosque" of Tabriz, was completed around 1465 under the Kara Koyunlu (Black Sheep) dynasty, the immediate predecessors of the Ak Koyunlu in Tabriz.[78] We can see not only deeply indented "star" medallions in repeat (fig. 14) but also lay-outs using small cartouches (fig. 15) in patterns that almost certainly inspired the designs of one of the "lesser-known" Ushak carpet types.[79]

Two things become clear from this discussion of the origins of some of the most important, early, Ushak carpet designs. The first is that the designers of the earliest Ushak carpets were participants in the overall development of the "international style" that permeated all of the arts in Anatolia along the Istanbul-Tabriz axis in the second half of the fifteenth century. The second is that, wherever else it may have been taking place, the carpet design revolution was happening in the carpets of Ushak in the second half of the fifteenth century with a vengeance, and the designs it produced formed an important pillar of the classical style in Anatolian carpets for centuries to come.

The impact of the early medallion Ushak carpets on the subsequent weaving of Anatolia was enormous. The medallion format continued to be woven in Ushak from the late fifteenth century to at least the late eighteenth century,[80] subject to evolution brought about by a changing knot ratio, stylization, and the economic decline of the Ushak manufactories. Because of the large size of many of the early examples, we have chosen to represent the entire tradition in this exhibition by one small and late example (cat. no. 35) that, although woven near the end of the tradition, preserves many of the forms and much of the brilliant coloration of the early examples. However, the enduring impact of the Ushak tradition was not confined to the familiar, large, medallion carpets. In addition to carpets woven in Ushak itself, many other areas in Anatolia produced carpets influenced by the classical Ushak prototypes.[81] Carpets in the medallion format, however, constitute a distinct minority among the hundreds of Ushak-influenced carpets woven in towns and villages of western, eastern, and central Anatolia in subsequent centuries. The reasons for this are not hard to find: medallion Ushaks are usually very large in size and their designs are difficult to copy due to their multitude of complex curvilinear forms, especially in the oak-leaf arabesques of the field. Unlike the simple geometry of a Lotto or Holbein carpet, which could be easily paraphrased by a village weaver, the medallion Ushaks presented an almost insurmountable challenge to a village weaver working on a small loom with a relatively low knot-count.

As a result, the impact of classical Ushak weaving comes not from the well-known medallion carpets but from other kinds of designs. In addition to the so-called "star" Ushak carpets with their comparatively simple designs of deeply indented, eight-lobed medallions and small, diamond-shaped cartouches (cat. no. 34), there are many other varieties. Some are characterized by eight-pointed medallions in what are, in effect, staggered rows (cat. no. 38).[82] Others (fig. 16)

Fig.14 (facing page) Tile decoration with design of repeated, indented, medallions Masjid-i Kabud, Tabriz, Iran, c. 1465
Photography courtesy of Abbas Daneshvari

Fig.15 (above) Tile decoration with design of small cartouches, Masjid-i Kabud, Tabriz, Iran, c. 1465
Photography courtesy of Abbas Daneshvari

Fig.16 "Four leaf clover" Ushak carpet
The Metropolitan Museum of Art
Gift of Joseph V. McMullan, 1972
(1972.80.4)
Photograph © 2002 The Metropolitan
Museum of Art

exhibit a simplified version of the "star" design, with a peculiar "four-leaf clover" arrangement of blue cartouches instead of deeply indented "star" medallions.[83] Although relatively rare, they had a much greater impact on later Anatolian weaving outside Ushak than any other Ushak design (cat. nos. 39–40). Also influenced by Ushak prototypes is another class of carpet, usually of a fairly large size, represented in the exhibition by catalogue number 37. In its blue-and-red coloration and the use of diamond-shaped small cartouche forms, it clearly belongs to the Ushak design tradition, although it was almost certainly woven in central or eastern Anatolia.

The longevity of the basic "medallion" and "star" types notwithstanding, by the sixteenth century the commercial manufactories of Ushak were capable of an astonishing range of inventiveness, and groups of newly recognized variants are still being published.[84] Occasionally, Ushak saw the production of carpets in highly original, small-scale, repeating patterns such as the lotus blossom arabesque in catalogue number 36. Out of the mainstream of Anatolian taste, and far too complex to have created descendants in Anatolian weaving, this carpet serves as a reminder that artistic inventiveness and commercial enterprise enjoyed a fruitful symbiotic relationship in the Ushak manufactories.

Carpet Designs and the Ottoman Court

We have suggested four "pillars" that form the basis of the classical style in the Anatolian carpet-weaving tradition. The last of these to be discussed is the Ottoman court style of Istanbul in the late sixteenth century. Attached to, and directly subsidized by the royal court in Istanbul the *nakkash-hane* (Turkish: *nakkaşhane*; literally: "place of design"), with its professional staff of salaried artists, was directly involved in executing royal artistic commissions in a variety of media. By the second half of the sixteenth century, and well into the seventeenth, carpets were woven under court control in ateliers both in Istanbul and in faraway Ottoman Cairo, following designs specifically created for carpet weavers by Istanbul court artists.[85]

Ottoman court carpets and court designs are the last of our four pillars to emerge chronologically. The origins of the Anatolian geometric carpets date back at least to the thirteenth century; if our hypothesis is correct, the classical textile sources for many later Anatolian carpet designs originate in the fifteenth century; Ushak carpets, as we have seen, may trace their origins back to the second half of the fifteenth century and to the appearance of the "carpet design revolution" in Anatolia. The distinctive Ottoman court style, however, did not emerge until the mid-sixteenth century, and the earliest Ottoman court carpets cannot be dated with much confidence to before 1570. By Ottoman court-style carpets we mean examples woven with court designs under court control in a distinctive technique and coloration, seen in this exhibition only in the fragments constituting catalogue number 20 and in the prayer carpet of catalogue number 44.

We have noted that the designs of medallion Ushak carpets were, due to their complexity, only rarely adapted by later Anatolian weavers and then usually in a radically simplified form. The same may be said in general of Ottoman court carpets. Certain design elements of court-carpet weaving did find their way from court carpets into Anatolian village carpets on a motif-by-motif basis. Perhaps the best known is the border seen on the Ballard prayer rug from The

Metropolitan Museum of Art (cat. no. 44). Composed of tulips with flanking leaves, carnations, and rosettes, it is also seen in a highly stylized form in a much later carpet (cat. no. 18), whose border was copied in turn from an eighteenth-century carpet, woven in Ladik in central Anatolia.[86] Another classical motif from court carpets, which finds its way into later Anatolian weaving, is the curved, serrated leaf. This motif, however, usually enters the Anatolian village repertoire not directly from Ottoman court carpets but rather from Ottoman velvet cushion covers, wall tiles, and other non-carpet media.[87]

By the end of the sixteenth century, the new court style was seen throughout the Ottoman Empire. Its impact was quickly felt in the media of silk textiles and the famous Iznik ceramics, with their white ground and brilliant colors. Growing out of the "international style" that had prevailed in the Ottoman Empire in the late fifteenth and early sixteenth centuries, the new Ottoman court style showed two distinctive aspects. The first was an arabesque of complex, stylized lotus flowers and curving, feather- or sword-like leaves attached to twisting vines. This was associated with the court artist Shah Kulu and is known today as the *saz* style, *saz* being an ancient Turkish term for a sort of enchanted forest.[88] The second is the repertoire of familiar Turkish garden flowers, such as tulips, carnations, hyacinths, rosebuds, and honeysuckles, developed in the mid-sixteenth century by Shah Kulu's talented pupil and successor, Kara Memi.[89] Because they were far easier to render in recognizable form in the carpet medium, the motifs associated with Kara Memi had a major impact on subsequent Anatolian weaving, appearing in hundreds of variegated forms throughout Anatolia. Combined with *saz* leaves on the border of the Ballard prayer rug (cat. no. 44), the tulips and carnations of the Kara Memi style then entered into the Anatolian repertoire as part of a very common border type. But in general the Kara Memi flowers only rarely appeared in the court carpets, and then usually in a minor role. When the classical, stylized flowers appear in most later Anatolian carpet weaving, like the *saz* leaf, they have entered the repertoire not from court carpets, but from silk textiles, embroidered textiles, and ceramics. This is especially true of Anatolian *yastık* rugs, many of which are paraphrases of silk-velvet *yastık* originals, which in turn took their floral motifs directly from professional textile designers who carefully adapted the latest trends from the court in Istanbul (cat. nos. 32–33).

In a very different vein, a group of long, narrow rugs woven in the eighteenth century or later, in or near the town of Karapınar in Konya province (cat. no. 42), also shows designs dominated by the floral repertoire, now heavily stylized and geometric in form. We know of no court carpets or Ushak carpets that might have served as prototypes for these distinctive and beautiful weavings, nor are there any known sources in embroidery or ceramics for the layouts and syntax of the forms. It is quite possible that we have here a local production that was invented by local weavers, using the court design repertoire in an entirely original manner for the sole purpose of making village carpets, which the weavers thought would be attractive in the marketplace. Whatever the sources, this group of Anatolian carpets, with its profound debt to the sixteenth-century classical court style, is one of the most attractive to have been produced in Anatolia.[90]

Finally, the white-ground Iznik tiles that were used to decorate Ottoman buildings had a powerful impact on commercial and village weaving in Anatolia. A group of Anatolian white-ground carpets, most of which are thought to originate in or near Ushak, curiously called "bird" carpets due to a misinterpretation of their geometrized leaf forms (cat. no. 41), are probably adapted in very simple form from an Iznik-tile prototype. The stencil-like disposition of the flowers is a common affectation of Iznik-tile designers in the 1550s and 1560s.[91] Another favorite Ottoman court motif, the three spots and two stripes known as *chinta-mani*, was adopted first in white-ground Ushak carpets, again probably directly from an Iznik-tile prototype,[92] and then subsequently appeared in various kinds of village carpets over the centuries.

Talisman and *Nazarlık*

To this point we have seen designs in Anatolian carpets whose origins can be attributed to the weaving technique itself, to nomadic tribal symbolism, and to the influence of other textile media such as silk textiles, architectural decoration, and the arts of the book. Occasionally we have also seen motifs that have served a quite specific function apart from the aesthetics of the design itself. In catalogue number 12 there are two small ornaments consisting of triangles with what appear to be small, hanging pendants. In catalogue number 22 a small ornament appears to "hang" from the upper end of the field in the carpet. And in the small *yastık* (cat. no. 30), we have seen at each end of the rug a row of small ornaments in pile technique, woven into the flat-woven *elem* or skirts. We have described all of these design elements as *nazarlık*, in effect small amulets added to carpet designs to protect the carpet itself and the carpet's owner from the "evil eye."

In many traditional societies one can find a popular mythology of an "evil eye"—some sort of evil spirit that seeks to mar or destroy goodness, beauty, symmetry, or artistic perfection out of spiteful envy. Tales abound in European folk-tales such as those collected by the Grimm brothers, with the curse placed by an evil witch on the infant Sleeping Beauty being perhaps the best-known example. In the Islamic world, the primary combatant against these evil forces is the written or spoken invocation *"Mashallah"*—"may God protect (it)." In Turkey, various symbols such as the *chintamani*, or various objects such as shiny silver jewelry with tiny hanging ornaments, or the ubiquitous blue-glass beads with an eye motif, have historically been used as amulets or "spirit scarecrows" to frighten off malign influences.

We should therefore not be at all surprised to see various motifs appearing in Anatolian carpets for this express purpose. However, such motifs, which are deliberately introduced into the carpet design for a specific apotropaic purpose, are not to be confused with the "intentional flaw" stories that used to be regularly told to customers by rug dealers. In the latter, any hiatus or "hiccup" in the design of a village or nomadic carpet would be explained as the deliberate attempt by the weaver to avoid perfection (which is for God alone), and thus to avoid the evil eye. Usually, a typical village or nomadic carpet contains not one but several of these "flaws," which as we have discussed (cat. no. 1) are a normal consequence of the artistic process of weaving, when the designer and weaver are the same person and both processes are undertaken simultaneously.

Sometimes *nazarlık* ornaments are introduced into a carpet design in such large numbers that they practically overwhelm that design.[93] In the exhibition, we have included one interesting carpet fragment from central Anatolia that contains depictions of jewelry with pendant elements, whose inaudible metaphoric metallic tinkling was thought to ward off the evil eye. Instead of the more common triangular shape, the weaver has chosen instead to depict these amulets, "hanging" both "up" and "down" in the design, as small decorated hexagons. While ornaments such as these are rarely found in very early carpets, they are commonly introduced by village or nomadic weavers into the descendants of classical prototypes in virtually every type of carpet, and every weaving area in Anatolia in the eighteenth and nineteenth centuries.

Anatolian Prayer Rugs

It would be fair to say that the prayer rugs of Anatolia are perhaps the best-known products of the Anatolian carpet-weaving tradition, in both flat-woven and pile-woven formats. Anatolian prayer rugs fall into two categories. Carpets from the first category, known as *saff*, are usually fairly large in size and consist of a number of compartments, each defining a space, usually around 100 by 150 cm (36 by 60 in). This space is suitable for one individual to perform the five daily Islamic prayers, which consist of recitation of Qur'anic verses and other prayers while standing, kneeling, and then for a brief time touching one's forehead to the carpet. *Saff* carpets were woven for use in mosques to serve as floor decoration, which helps to facilitate during prayers the lining up of worshippers in long ranks side by side as they face the *mihrab* or niche that indicates the direction of the *qiblah* in a mosque. The compartments in a *saff* carpet frequently exhibit a point or an arch at one end, indicating the direction faced during prayer. The form of this arch may suggest either the *mihrab* or a doorway, which symbolizes the gateway to Paradise. Some *saff* carpets define their compartments with a design of an architectural arcade—row after row of arches on columns—which may actually represent the arches and columns of the mosque itself. Often *saff* carpets include decorative motifs such as flowers, symbolizing the gardens of Paradise, or hanging lamps, symbolizing God's divine light. They also may include indications of where the worshippers' feet are to be placed. Small ornamental rugs in *saff* form, usually meant for decorative use as wall hangings and with compartments far too small to accommodate individual worshippers, are not properly to be considered as prayer rugs.[94]

The second category of prayer rug is known as *sajjadah* (modern Turkish: *seccade*), an Arabic word meaning "for prostration," or *namazlık*, a Persian/Turkish word meaning "for prayer". These are small rugs, around 150–175 by 100–125 cm (59–69 by 39–49 in), and are intended either for floor-use by one individual during prayer, or to be hung on a wall in a space devoted to prayer to serve as a symbolic *mihrab*.[95] In decoration and iconography, *sajjadah* rugs demonstrate much the same range of motifs and symbolism as *saff* carpets. *Sajjadah* rugs are especially favored among village weavers, because their small size requires a fairly small loom, and the time interval between the purchase of the raw materials and the selling of the finished product is fairly short, so that the weaver's investment in materials is not tied up for a great deal of time.

In Anatolia, both types of prayer rugs, the large *saff* and the small *sajjadah*, can be further divided into several basic design types, with particular kinds of decoration and iconography.[96] The most common type shows a plain, single-color central field with an indication of directionality at one end; such rugs were woven in great numbers in Anatolian villages over the centuries. Another common type depicts the central space under the arch, filled with plant and floral motifs, which symbolize the gardens of Paradise promised in the next life to true believers; their spectrum ranges from simple village carpets to one-of-a-kind masterpieces, created in court-controlled workshops for royal use. Yet another type incorporates architectural motifs, such as a single column on either side under the arch or two pairs of coupled columns supporting three arches, sometimes with additional columns to either side. That design, used all over Anatolia through the centuries, apparently stems from a classical prototype created for the Ottoman court in Istanbul in the late sixteenth century.[97] Some prayer rugs indicate by foot-shaped forms at the bottom of the arch the place where the worshipper's feet should be placed during prayer, while others show images of hands at the top of the rug, indicating where hands should be placed during prostration.[98] A very few *sajjadahs* show under the arch a simple dark square, which is meant to be a depiction of the Kaaba, the cubical building in Mecca believed by Muslims to have been built by the prophet Ibrahim (Abraham), toward which all Muslims face during prayer.[99]

All of these types of prayer rugs have been woven in Anatolia for the past four centuries, and all have been extensively documented and discussed in the rug literature. Certain artistic forms quite distinctive to Anatolia may reflect the indigenous architectural forms of that country. For example, the stepped, steeply pointed "arches", seen at the top of so many different types of village prayer rugs, mirror the stepped tops of *mihrab* niches in Anatolian mosques, and are filled with the honeycomb- or stalactite-like geometrical three-dimensional arabesque known as *muqarnas* (fig. 17).[100] Another explanation for the prevalence of these stepped-arch forms in Anatolian prayer rugs is that the vast majority of Anatolian rugs exhibit some degree of vertical "squashing" of forms, resulting from widely spaced warps and packed knotting, and thus their diagonals are not very steep, often no more than 40 degrees from the horizontal. Thus, in order to get a steeply directional "point" at the "top" of a prayer rug, the use of steps much taller than they are wide may compensate for the lack of an easy way for the weaver to make a steep diagonal in her design.

Another unusual feature of Anatolian prayer rugs is the fact that large numbers of them were woven "upside down"—that is, the weaver began weaving at the top of the design. On some occasions, this phenomenon appears to result from a complete ignorance on the part of the weaver as to the meaning of the design she was weaving. If the "arch" of such a rug is placed at the top of the field of view, small decorative forms that may have been added by the weaver to the rug design, such as bunches of flowers, small water pitchers, or even little animal figures, will then appear upside down.[101] More commonly, however, there is a very practical, technical reason for a weaver to begin a prayer rug from the top of the design. In terms of the pattern, weaving the bottom of a *sajjadah*, especially an Anatolian one, is "uncomplicated". The field of the typical Anatolian prayer rug is frequently of one color and is usually squared at the bottom, without any ornament. By contrast, the design of the top of a prayer rug is usually very complex, with an arch form consisting of two converging lines of pattern that eventually meet in the middle to form an "arch" or point. Other frequent features include decorated, triangular spandrels to either side of the arch, a depiction of a hanging lamp in the field, and a panel of flowers or some other form of ornament above the "arch."

Because of the complexity of these forms at the top of the rug, it was not always possible for a weaver to calculate the place at which the converging lines of the arch from each side would eventually meet and thus to determine when to

Fig.17 Tiled *mihrab* of the mosque of Eşref Oğlu, Beyşehir, late 13th century
Photography by Walter B. Denny

begin creating the complex top part of the design in the weaving process. On the very small looms normally used for *sajjadah* weaving, weavers often ran out of warp yarns and were forced to finish the upper end of a rug quite perfunctorily, sometimes with a too-narrow border, and at other times by omitting blossoms on a row of flower stems.[102] Weaving the rug upside down, starting with the top or complicated part of the design, made this problem much easier to solve. As she came to within an easily definable border's-width of the end of the loom, the weaver could simply weave a horizontal "bottom" border and finish her project quickly, using as much of the warp strung on her loom as possible. If working for an entrepreneur who paid according to the size or number of knots in the rug, this system allowed her to get the most area—and therefore money—for each rug. Because the direction of their pile points up, thus diminishing their reactivity to light from above, to display "upside-down" rugs on a wall to maximum advantage can be both difficult and frustrating. But from the weaver's point of view, the results were both beautiful and practical, and parochial notions of "right side up" and "upside down" were largely irrelevant for a rug meant to be used on the floor.

The most distinctive and complex of Anatolian prayer rugs are the examples that depict three arches and show pairs of very slender columns dividing the central arched space from the two lateral spaces. As mentioned, these appear to stem from a very specific prototype (cat. no. 44), a type of Ottoman court prayer rug woven in the second half of the sixteenth century. This type of carpet has survived in only one example, given by James Ballard to The Metropolitan Museum of Art, which can be dated to the last third of the sixteenth century.[103] In every century since the sixteenth, Turkish weavers have turned to the coupled-column prototype and its numerous descendants for inspiration. The chain of stylization from the prototype to village weavings of the late nineteenth century is one of the most fascinating art-historical metamorphoses in the Islamic world.[104] In the exhibition we have reconstructed this metamorphosis, from the Ballard prayer rug itself (cat. no. 44) to the seventeenth-century coupled-column "church rug" (cat. no. 46, a type found in significant numbers in churches in central Europe), through a magnificent early eighteenth-century "proto-Ladik" carpet collected by George Hewitt Myers (cat. no. 47), to a coupled-column village rug (cat. no. 49), and ending with the vertical symmetry of two "double-ended" examples (cat. nos. 51–52). The gradual metamorphosis of the coupled-column design is a fascinating story, but it does not pose much of a mystery. A sophisticated architectural idea, replete with Corinthian columns, faceted column bases, a parapet with flowers between the crenellations, small *rumi* split-leaf forms in the arch spandrels, and small domes on top of three half-round arches, gradually changes into a more formulaic type of rug. Finally, it succumbs to the creativity of village weavers who knew almost nothing of columns and arches, but a great deal about color, and whose desire for top-to-bottom symmetry obliterates both the form and the meaning of the original design.

However, there is another story behind these carpets, which is a great deal more of a mystery—the story of their artistic genesis and meaning. For at the out-set we have to note that in the entire history of Ottoman architecture, from the fourteenth century onward, there is neither a tradition of slender-paired columns nor is there any tradition of faceted-column bases, nor round arches such as these. With the exception of the small domes atop the parapet in the Ballard prayer rug, there is nothing in its architectural imagery that reflects actual

Ottoman architecture. To be sure, the main border, with its tulips, carnations, rosettes, hyacinths, and feather-like curved and serrated leaves, reflects the court style of the late sixteenth century. It combines two major currents in late sixteenth-century Ottoman court art: the sinuous *saz* leaves redolent of a mysterious enchanted forest of Turkic mythology, and the beloved Ottoman garden flowers made popular by the great artist Kara Memi after the middle of the sixteenth century.[105] But the architecture of the rug is an enigma. How can we explain it?

There are several possible approaches. We know that the technique of the Ottoman court carpets, as well as many of the most celebrated Ottoman court carpets themselves, come from Egypt in the year 1585. A decree from Sultan Murad III ordered the Ottoman governor of Cairo to send six weavers and a large quantity of dyed wool to the Ottoman court in Istanbul.[106] Could the source of the architecture in the Ballard carpet lie in Egypt? In Egypt, there are indeed coupled columns to be found in Islamic architecture, but they belong to much older monuments constructed in the Fatimid period, when recycled classical columns and capitals were doubled up in order to support the heavy imposts of Fatimid arches in the eleventh-century mosque of al-Azhar. The search for parallels to the Ballard prayer rug's coupled columns and triple arches in the architecture of Egypt bears little more fruit than a search among the monuments of the Ottomans in Turkey. The same holds true for spandrels, capitals, merlons, and crenellations.

Another possibility for the origin of the imagery of the Ballard prayer rug could be that it represents a distilled version of a *saff* carpet, perhaps an ancestor of the coupled-column *saff* carpet fragment in the exhibition (cat. no. 49). We might see the Ballard prayer rug as an attempt to take a design of three niches or compartments from a *saff* and combine them in one very small prayer rug, thus reflecting the iconography of the hypostyle or many-columned Arab mosque in this Ottoman court carpet. The idea is intriguing, but it still does not explain the coupled columns. More likely is the possibility that the three arches symbolize a triple gateway to Paradise, a concept already well established in Islamic art.[107]

What about pre-Ottoman architecture in Anatolia, closer to home? Looking back to Seljuk times in Anatolia, we do indeed see some delicate columns with Corinthian-like capitals in a series of monuments built and decorated by Syrian artists in the first half of the thirteenth century. Highly ornamented columns with similar leafy capitals appear on the outer doorway of the Sultanhan caravansaray on the Konya-Aksaray road (1228), and on either side of the doorway to the Karatay Medrese in Konya, built around 1250 (fig. 18). But these are single columns and they support no arches—they are decorative ornaments on carved marble façades.

In fact, there is one place in the Islamic world, with architecture that bears significant resemblance to that of the Ballard prayer rug. It is far away at the other end of the Mediterranean, in the Spanish hilltop palace of the Nasrid dynasty in Granada, known as the Alhambra (fig. 19). The small garden pavilions in the famous Court of the Lions, completed in the fourteenth century, show a use of slender coupled columns in a triple-arch context, albeit in a different order than that of the Ballard prayer rug. However, the resemblance is striking and on its face suggests a relationship between the two. But by the time of the weaving of the Ballard prayer rug, Granada had been incorporated into the Catholic realm of Castile and Aragon for almost a century. What possible connection could there

Fig. 18 Detail of *girih* arabesque and small columns, west facade, Karatay Medrese, Konya, *c.* 1250
Photography by Walter B. Denny

Fig.19 Garden pavilion, Court of the
Lions, Alhambra, Granada, mid-
14th century
Photography by Walter B. Denny

be then between a fourteenth-century Islamic monument in Spain and an
Ottoman court carpet, probably woven near Istanbul in the 1570s or 1580s?

In fact, the hypothesis that the design of the Ballard prayer rug may have
something to do with Spain is not as far-fetched as it may seem. After all, by
1600, copies of Turkish carpets had been produced in Spain under Muslim and
Christian patronage alike for around 200 years; if artistic ideas could travel from
east to west, then why not in the opposite direction? At the beginning of the
sixteenth century, the Ottoman cities of Istanbul, Salonika, and Sarajevo had
begun to welcome thousands of Spanish-speaking refugees fleeing from the
Inquisition and the intolerance of Andalusia's new Catholic rulers. The refugee
communities grew and flourished, and some of their leaders rose to positions
of great prominence in the multiethnic and multicultural Ottoman society.
These were the Sephardic Jews of the Ottoman Empire, in whose Istanbul neigh-
borhoods the fifteenth-century Spanish dialect known as Ladino can still be
heard today.

But what would Sephardic Jews have to do with the imagery of an Ottoman
court rug destined for the Ottoman sultan or his family, and woven to further the
practice of the five daily prayers mandated by the religion of Islam? The roots of
part of the answer may go back over 250 years before the Ballard prayer rug was
created, to a collection of fourteenth-century documents known to scholars as

responsa, associated with the eminent rabbinical authority Asher ben Yehiel, who lived in Spain between 1304 and 1327.[108] The documents consist of questions about Jewish religious practice, which were posed by representatives of various congregations to Rabbi Asher, together with the rabbi's answer (*responsum*) to each question. One question arose as the result of certain synagogues following the practice of covering the Torah ark with a carpet that served as a *parokhet* or curtain. Someone noticed that this carpet had a design of a black square that might indicate a Muslim iconography, making the carpet inappropriate for use as a *parokhet*, and they wrote to the rabbi asking an opinion. The rabbi replied that indeed these suspicions were correct: the black square (as we have seen, a depiction of the Kaaba in Mecca) was indeed a Muslim symbol, and the rug in question should not be used as a *parokhet*. The same question of appropriate use of Muslim *sajjadah* in a synagogue arose again in the time of Asher's son Rabbi Judah (d. 1349), who received a similar question from his own nephew, also a rabbi.[109] These incidents are interesting in that they show the blurring of cultural boundaries between Islam and Judaism in the use of Islamic carpets in a Jewish liturgical setting as early as the beginning of the fourteenth century.

The origin of the fourteenth-century Muslim *sajjadah* with a Kaaba depiction remains a mystery, but the earliest surviving prayer rug with such a depiction, probably from the seventeenth or eighteenth century, is an Anatolian carpet that is today in the Museum of Turkish and Islamic Art in Istanbul.[110]

In fact, the use of an Islamic pile carpet in a synagogue was apparently not an unusual custom. One of the well-known carpets in The Textile Museum's collections is a seventeenth-century Ottoman *parokhet* in *sajjadah* form, woven from S-spun wool, probably in a court-manufactory in Ottoman-controlled Egypt (cat. no. 45). It reflects a well-known type of court *sajjadah*, with a single arch supported by decorated single or coupled columns to either side of the field, and faceted bases that appear to be rendered in perspective. To this form is added a central motif of a *menorah* in the form of a chalice decorated with nine hanging lamps. In a panel above the arch is a Hebrew inscription from the book of Psalms CXVIII : 20—"This is the Gate of the Lord: Through it the Righteous Enter." Not only is the form similar to that of Ottoman court *sajjadahs*[111] but the iconography of a gateway to heaven is the same as well. This carpet, made in a court-controlled workshop for a synagogue, testifies to the continued intermingling of Jewish and Islamic artistic traditions in the carpet medium. Another very similar example is found in the Wolfson Collection in the National Museum, Jerusalem.[112]

An even more astonishing discovery was made in recent years. The Italian carpet historian Alberto Boralevi found, in the possession of a synagogue in Padua in northern Italy, a *parokhet* in *sajjadah* size and format. This carpet was woven in S-spun Egyptian wool using a fifteenth- or sixteenth-century Mamluk technique and border design, with a field design of an arch encompassing a flaming brazier, and flanked by two Ionic pilasters shown in perspective (fig. 20).[113] It presents us with an intermixture of Jewish epigraphy and iconography; Egyptian Muslim materials, technique, and border design; an Italianate architectural rendering in linear perspective; and a depiction of flames derived from a motif known as *chintamani*, which was very prevalent in classical Ottoman Turkish art.[114] At the top of the composition is the same inscription found on The Textile Museum rug—"This is the Gate of the Lord: Through it the Righteous Enter."

Fig. 20 *Parokhet* carpet from the Padua Synagogue, probably Egypt or Italy, late 15th century

These fifteenth- and sixteenth-century "classical" *parokhet* spawned artistic offspring over the centuries in the same way that the classical Anatolian carpets did. The Jewish Museum in New York has two nineteenth-century knotted-pile *parokhet* in *sajjadah* form, one from a central Anatolian village and another from Gördes in western Anatolia, both almost certainly woven for synagogue use on commission by Muslim weavers.[115] The latter rug (cat. no. 48) has even more complex iconography, including a Jewish adaptation of the Muslim "hand" forms and a beautifully drawn single lamp under the arch, together with the now-familiar inscription from Psalm CXVIII : 20.

The goal of discussing these Islamic carpets adapted for Jewish ritual use, is to suggest that the design of the Ballard prayer rug may reflect a complex Mediterranean synthesis unique to the sixteenth century. This includes elements of Ottoman court design (the borders and the flowers in the field), Ottoman architecture (the small domes above the parapet), Ottoman adaptations of Egyptian dyeing and weaving techniques (the materials and construction), Islamic iconography (the hanging lamp and the triple gateway to Paradise), Italian one-point perspective (the column bases), and an adaptation of Spanish Islamic architectural forms that traveled east (slender coupled columns), perhaps in the form of a now-lost embroidered or woven *parokhet* brought to the Ottoman Empire by Jewish refugees. These elements came together to form a classical prototype for literally hundreds of Anatolian *sajjadahs* (as well as a number of Torah curtains) over the subsequent centuries. This is a complex story, but it is a story supported by the available evidence, and it explains better than any other the genesis of the Ballard prayer rug and its numerous and varied artistic descendants.

Conclusion: Historical Perspectives and Anatolian Carpets

The intent of this exhibition and its accompanying catalogue is to demonstrate the profound debt owed by many generations of Anatolian weavers to a classical past that helped to define the general artistic parameters under which most Anatolian carpets of the past four centuries were woven.

Beyond that, it serves to emphasize that vital artistic traditions, full of originality and beauty, can exist within the framework of a profound debt to tradition. In these carpets we see proof that between tradition and originality there is no essential conflict, but the possibility of a profound symbiosis: the carpet art of the nineteenth century illuminates that of the sixteenth in much the same way as the carpet art of the sixteenth century illuminates that of the nineteenth.

The works of art in the exhibition also demonstrate another profound truth that is often overlooked in our times, and that has to do with modes of artistic learning. Those responsible for the design of these carpets (cat. nos. 20, 44, 45, and possibly 48) were probably men; the gender of the weavers is uncertain. Women wove most of the other carpets in the exhibition, and most of the original variations on the basic theme that they manifest were largely created by the weavers in their dual capacity as designers. A few of these carpets were woven according to written instructions or graphic models; the bulk, however, were woven either from memory or as adaptations of other, older carpets that each weaver/designer may have placed in front of herself to guide her as she wove and created her own designs. In late nineteenth-century France, artists argued violently over the value of formal training and the role of the academy in the education of artists. In the case of the Anatolian weaving tradition, such an argument is supremely irrelevant, for once the technical threshold is attained by a young girl working at the side of her mother, aunt, or older sister, the artistic path is wide open. These women weavers, mostly illiterate and with no formal schooling, and with no academic knowledge of their own history beyond the tribal legends and village traditions they learned from their parents, created art of powerful originality and visual impact within the embrace of a strong tradition, each enhancing the other. For us in the twenty-first century, it should be both an enlightening and a humbling experience to confront the results of their labors.

Key to terms, abbreviations, and organization

Design

Sometimes a carpet is woven with the intention that its design be viewed from an orientation other than that of the actual physical bottom (beginning of weaving) and top (end of weaving) of the carpet. In such cases, we illustrate the carpet in the proper viewing orientation, but note the actual top and bottom in the catalogue entry. Otherwise, all carpets are illustrated with the top and bottom as woven.

Colors

Names or descriptions of colors are necessarily subjective, but have been kept as simple as possible.

Our lists of colors attempt to describe the intent of the dyer. Variations in the dyers' hues, known as *abrash*, are almost always present, and where *abrash* leads to significant variation in hue it is noted in the list of colors. Some dyestuffs may be corrosive, causing pile in that color to wear badly or even to disappear completely, especially the black-brown dyed yarn used for outlining in many Anatolian rugs. This feature is noted where present, and occasionally the more unusual non-corroded black-brown is mentioned where significant.

Dimensions

Warp (vertical) dimensions are given before weft (horizontal) dimensions, centimeters are given before inches (1 inch has been computed as 2.54 centimeters).

As the dimensions of carpets change with temperature, humidity, stretching, and hanging, all given dimensions are to be construed as approximate.

Fiber make-up

Z-spun = clockwise spun
S-spun = counter-clockwise spun
Weft shoots are alternate unless otherwise noted
// = two one-ply weft yarns employed parallel to each other

Knot density

The use of the decimeter (10 centimeters, equivalent to 3.94 inches, abbreviated dm) as the basic unit measuring knot density is preferable in very coarsely or irregularly woven carpets.

As the vertical and horizontal numbers of knots in a decimeter constitute important information, while the actual number of knots in a given area is usually of little interest, we have listed the coordinates of knot density, but have not given their multiplied product. For those interested in the knots-per-area statistic, 1 square decimeter is computed as 15.52 square inches, and 1 square inch is computed as 0.064 square decimeters.

Publication references

Publications are not listed exhaustively; previous publications are cited where they contain additional information or are otherwise pertinent.

For an explanation of how and why carpet analysis is undertaken, see Denny and Walker 1988, pp. 63–69.

Detail of a Ghirlandaio-pattern carpet, western or northwestern Anatolia, probably 18th or 19th century (cat. no. 17)

3
"CHESSBOARD" OR "DAMASCUS" CARPET

Probably Syria, late 16th century
The Textile Museum R34.34.1
Acquired by George Hewitt Myers in 1927
377 × 243 cm (149 × 95¹/₂ in)

This carpet is typical of a group of rugs now
thought to be the product of Syrian looms
in the 16th and 17th centuries. They share
characteristically asymmetrical knots open to
the left, warp yarns crowded together in two
levels, and the very stiff but lustrous wool
seen in this example, which does not hold its
spin well. The second characteristic causes
the design to appear "stretched" vertically,
rather than the more common vertical
"squashing" caused by widely spaced warp
yarns, and strenuously packed knots and
wefts (cat. no. 1). The main motif is an eight-
pointed *girih* or "knotted" strapwork star.
The same motif is seen in pairs in each
compartment of the Anatolian *saff*
carpet (cat. no. 2); in this case the star is
surrounded by sixteen elongated "dart"
motifs and small flowers.

The majority of "Damascus" carpets
known today exhibit the so-called chessboard design of the present example, the
name evidently being an allusion to the
organization of the field in squares. Some
authors have commented on the peculiar
term "chessboard" that is used to describe
this design, and which actually appears in old
documents as an indication of carpet design
as well (Pinner 1986). The term is more
puzzling in this context because there are
actually carpets with designs that far more
closely resemble chessboards (cat. no. 7;
Ölçer and Denny 1999, pls. 26–27).

Published: Kühnel and Bellinger 1957, p. 75

WARP: wool: off-white (undyed), stiff, 2 Z-spun
yarns plied S; alternate warps depressed

WEFT: wool: brownish red, stiff, 1 Z-spun yarn;
2 shoots

PILE: wool: dark red, light blue, light blue-green,
dark blue, black-brown, yellow varying shades
from light yellow to brownish yellow (*abrash*),
off-white (undyed), 2 Z-spun yarns plied S

asymmetrical knot open left, V 28–29 ×
H 34–40 per dm (7–7¹/₂ × 8¹/₂ –10 per in)

EDGES: cut
ENDS: cut, taped

Analysis by Charles Grant Ellis and
Walter B. Denny

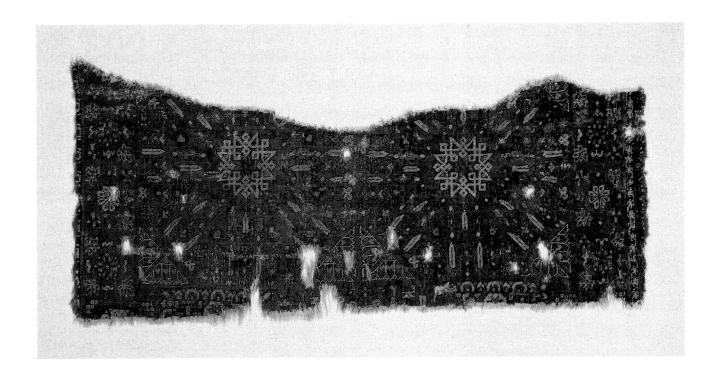

4
"PARA-MAMLUK" CARPET FRAGMENT

Possibly Azerbaijan, Tabriz in northwestern Iran,
15th or early 16th century
The Textile Museum R34.32.1
Acquired by George Hewitt Myers in 1953
45 × 98 cm (18 × 38 1/2 in)

Only a small number of the so-called para-Mamluk carpets and fragments have survived, most in quite small sizes, but the influence of the group on subsequent weaving in the Mediterranean countries has been enormous. The characteristics of the group include designs based on complex *girih* geometric forms, including what we call a "strapwork star," an eight-pointed star-like form that appears to be interlaced from one continuous ribbon or strap, and an "early" kufesque border patterned on Arabic calligraphy. The eight-pointed "knotted" strapwork stars seen in this fragment are surrounded by stylized blossoms and "dart" forms, which are seen also in catalogue number 3 and in an important group of early Cairene carpets. These carpets exhibit an almost perfect 1:1 knot ratio, leading to radially symmetrical forms. While all three depictions of carpets from this group in Italian painting date to the 16th century (Ellis 1988, pp. 5–7), there are strong reasons

for attributing the group as a whole to the 15th century.

Carpets such as these may well have been the "Tabriz" carpets noted by Barbaro in 1474, which he thought to be superior to those of Bursa and Cairo. They were probably conceived at the court of the Ak Koyunlu (White Sheep) Türkmen rulers in Tabriz, and woven in very small numbers in an atelier under the direct control of the court. They appear to be the inspiration for slightly later carpets woven in Egypt, Syria, and Anatolia. Some of them are very closely allied in design with the earliest carpets of the large-pattern Holbein group. In many respects they represent the apogee of geometric carpet design before the "carpet design revolution" of the late 15th century, a phenomenon that probably also began in Azerbaijan and Anatolia.

Published: Kühnel and Bellinger 1957, p. 77;
Spuhler 1986, p. 267

WARP: wool: off-white (undyed), 2 Z-spun yarns plied S; alternate warps depressed

WEFT: wool: red, one Z-spun yarn; 2 shoots

PILE: wool: red, light blue, green, white (undyed), black-brown, 2 Z-spun yarns plied S

asymmetrical knot open left, V 55 × H 55 per dm (14 × 14 per in)

EDGES: cut

ENDS: cut

Analysis by Charles Grant Ellis

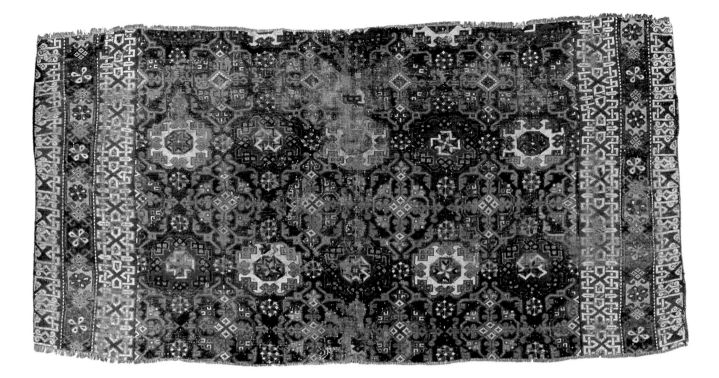

5
SMALL-PATTERN HOLBEIN
CARPET FRAGMENT

Central Anatolia, probably early 15th century
The Textile Museum R34.17.2
Acquired by George Hewitt Myers in 1928
121 × 237 cm (47 1/2 × 93 in)

Small-pattern Holbein carpets take their name from a carpet depicted on a table in Holbein's early 16th-century portrait of the Hanseatic merchant Georg Gisze, in the Berlin Museums. This style of carpets is depicted in many other European paintings as well (Ellis 1986). In terms of design, the earliest surviving example is a fragment in the Museum of Turkish and Islamic Art in Istanbul (TIEM Inv. No. 303, illustrated in Ölçer, Enderlein, Batári, and Mills 1996, pl. 50). The earliest example depicted in a painting is found in an altarpiece, *The Madonna Enthroned*, by Andrea Mantegna in the church of San Zeno, Verona, dated between 1457 and 1459. A magnificent Spanish copy datable to the 15th century is found in the MFA, Boston (No. 39.614), as further evidence of the early export of carpets of this type to Europe (Denny 1978, p. 159).

The Textile Museum fragment, although it does not have the 1:1 knot ratio of the earliest known examples, is certainly from one of the older carpets of this type known to us. As a

large carpet, originally around 600–750 cm (240–288 in) long, its design consists of stacked rows of five characteristic knotted strapwork *gül*, which alternate in coloration from blue strapwork on a red background to black-brown strapwork (now corroded) on white. Where the black-brown knotting has disappeared, the white background jumps out to the eye. In later descendants of this design, the confusion of the motif (the strap-work) and the background color (the red or white) often leads to the ground becoming a motif and the original motif being lost altogether. The secondary motif is a quatrefoil, defined by eight split-leaf or *rumi* forms that constitute its outer contours.

The most archaic of the small-pattern Holbein carpets such as this one, frequently exhibit a calligraphic kufesque outer border and a plaited kufesque inner border. Between the two red-ground borders is a third border, consisting of eight-petalled flowers in cartouches, each with two hooks at the end. This border serves a link between the earliest

Anatolian classical carpets and more recent Türkmen weaving of central Asia, where borders such as this are termed *ashyk* (knucklebone). The motif may well have been brought to Anatolia from Central Asia in the 12th or 13th century (Denny 1982).

Published: Mackie 1974, no. 25

WARP: wool: off-white (undyed), 2 Z-spun yarns plied S; alternate warps slightly depressed

WEFT: wool: red, 1 Z-spun yarn; 2 shoots; discontinuous wefts cause pattern of diagonals (lazy lines) on back of carpet

PILE: wool: blue-green varying in shade to blue (*abrash*), medium blue, light blue, red, dark red, light yellow, orange, off-white (undyed), black-brown (corroded), 2 Z-spun yarns plied S

symmetrical knot, V 23–25 × H 18 per dm (6 × 4 1/2 per in)

EDGES: cut

ENDS: cut

Analysis by Charles Grant Ellis

6
SMALL-PATTERN HOLBEIN CARPET

Probably central Anatolia, probably 16th century
The Textile Museum R34.17.1
Acquired by George Hewitt Myers in 1928
213 × 150 cm (84 × 59 in)

Small-pattern Holbein carpets were woven over a period of more than two centuries, appearing in many variations and gradually tending toward a design that was more compacted vertically. The blue ground of this example is more typical than the rectangular compartment layout of catalogue number 7, and the individual *gül* forms are about half as wide as they are high due to the structure of the weave. This 16th-century example shows a border that has evolved from the white-on-red calligraphic kufesque of the earliest 15th-century examples, through the lattice of the early 16th-century examples seen in catalogue number 5, into a variant with diagonal plaits in which the vestigial letter finials now point both in and out.

Published: Mackie 1974, no. 26

WARP: wool: off-white (undyed), 2 Z-spun yarns plied S; alternate warps slightly depressed

WEFT: wool: red, 1 Z-spun yarn; 2 shoots, sometimes 3 (2 // + 1); discontinuous wefts cause pattern of diagonals (lazy lines) on back of carpet

PILE: wool: dark red, orange-red, dark blue varying in shade to light blue (*abrash*), off-white (undyed), light yellow, black-brown, 2 Z-spun yarns plied S

symmetrical knot, V 43–44 × H 26–31 per dm (11–11$^{1}/_{2}$ × 6$^{1}/_{2}$ –8 per in)

EDGES: cut

ENDS: bottom: 0.5 cm red tapestry weave using dark red weft, stripped; top: stripped

Analysis by Charles Grant Ellis and Walter B. Denny

7
SMALL-PATTERN HOLBEIN CARPET

Central Anatolia, probably 15th century
Marshall and Marilyn R. Wolf Collection
249 × 211 cm (98 × 83 in)

This attractive example is organized in rectangular compartments, giving different colored backgrounds for the rows of *güls*. Extensively cut and pieced, it maintains its approximate original width, but has been shortened to less than half of its original length.

The variations in color divide the secondary quatrefoil motifs in four, and give them the appearances of cornerpieces in the individual squares. The border is a typical example of the "plaited kufesque" type, found in many such carpets depicted in 16th-century European painting.

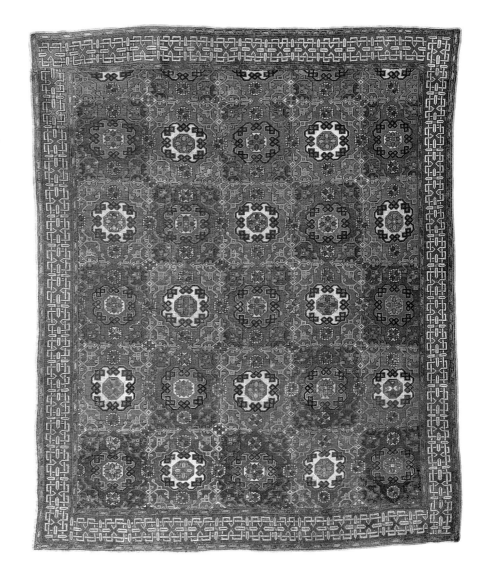

WARP: wool: off-white (undyed), 2 Z-spun yarns plied S; alternate warps slightly depressed

WEFT: wool: red, 1 Z-spun yarn; 2 shoots

PILE: wool: light green, blue-green, medium blue, light blue, light red, dark brown-red, off-white (undyed), black-brown (corroded), 2 Z-spun yarns plied S

symmetrical knot, 39 × 36 per dm (10 × 9 per in)

EDGES: cut

ENDS: cut

Analysis by Louise W. Mackie

8
SMALL-PATTERN HOLBEIN DERIVATIVE CARPET

Probably western Anatolia, 18th or 19th century
Marshall and Marilyn R. Wolf Collection
183 × 130 cm (72 × 51 in)

The countless variations on small-pattern Holbein designs, which exist in later carpets, can be found in weavings from every corner of Anatolia. This example shows six red star-like forms that on close examination show traces of the strapwork knot elements seen in the small-pattern Holbein *gül*, which penetrate the red forms from four directions. The red forms are a result of the phenomenon of ground-motif confusion, in which the background of a design motif, such as the white background of the *güls* in catalogue number 5, becomes a design motif in its own right. We see this phenomenon again and again in the fascinating process of evolution in Anatolian carpet designs.

WARP: wool: off-white (undyed), some brown- and white-wool yarns plied together, 2 Z-spun yarns plied S; one level

WEFT: wool: red, 1 Z-spun yarn; 2–3 shoots

PILE: wool: red, blue, blue-green, yellow, purple, white (undyed), black-brown (slightly corroded), 2 Z-spun yarns plied S

symmetrical knot, V 18 × H 18 per dm
(4 $^1/_2$ × 4 $^1/_2$ per in)

EDGES: restored

ENDS: approximately 9 cm of red-and-blue striped tapestry weave at both ends, stripped

Analysis by Walter B. Denny and
Sumru Belger Krody

9

SMALL-PATTERN HOLBEIN DERIVATIVE CARPET

Probably western Anatolia, 18th or 19th century
From a Massachusetts Collector
147 × 127 cm (58 × 50 in)

This carpet shows startling color changes as the weaver ran out of green and then out of light-blue pile yarn at the top of the rug. The ten repeating motifs are probably not derived directly from the small-pattern Holbein *gül*, but from a similar geometric octagonal motif. The balance between motif and ground is intriguing. At times, the hooked elements of what appears to be the ground of each rectangular compartment predominate, while at other times the two-part octagonal motif appears to be the major design element.

WARP: wool: off-white (undyed), 2 Z-spun yarns plied S; one level

WEFT: wool: red, 1 Z-spun yarn; 2–4 shoots, occasionally 6 shoots

PILE: wool: dark red, light orange, light blue, green, yellow, medium purple, off-white (undyed), black-brown (corroded and uncorroded), 2 Z-spun yarns plied S

symmetrical knot, V 24 × H 20 per dm
(6 × 5 per in)

EDGES: flat selvedge of 5 warp yarns with red weft, over-wrapped with 2 colors of pile yarn

ENDS: stripped

Analysis by Walter B. Denny

10

SMALL-PATTERN HOLBEIN DERIVATIVE RUG

Probably from central or south-central Anatolia, 19th century

Collection of Jon M. and Deborah Anderson

198 × 127 cm (78 × 50 in)

The long pile, the extremely coarse and irregular weave, and the appearance of this carpet with its extra end panels or *elem*, might lead one to think that it is a small *yastık* face or cushion face. In fact, it is a large, heavy, thick rug, created with a relatively small amount of weaving labor and a relatively large amount of wool; this suggests that it might have served as a *yatak* or mattress rug.

The nine motifs in the field are stretched vertically by the large number of weft shoots, although the weave varies a great deal, and in most of the rug the ratio of vertical to horizontal knots is around 3:2, giving very steep diagonals. These motifs, vastly simplified from earlier motifs seen in the small-pattern Holbein *gül* of catalogue numbers 6 and 7, are similar to those found in catalogue number 9, but the lack of square compartments eliminates any balance between ground and motif. The original classical motif has metamorphosed entirely into the plain-red background, leaving only the backgrounds of the proto-type, which have now been transformed into motifs themselves.

WARP: wool: white (undyed), some brown- and white-wool yarns plied together, 2 Z-spun yarns plied S; one level

WEFT: wool: off-white (undyed), yellow and red, 1 Z-spun yarn; 2-12 shoots

goat hair: black-brown, 1 Z-spun yarn; usually 2 shoots

PILE: wool: red, yellow, green, blue, dark brown, white (undyed), 2 Z-spun yarns plied S

symmetrical knot, V 12–15 × H 16–17 per dm (3–4 × 4–4^{1}/$_{2}$ per in)

EDGES: flat selvedge of 4 bundles of 2 warp yarns woven with white, red, yellow, and dark brown wefts

ENDS: 1 cm yellow tapestry weave, a single line of red-and-white weft-twining over 2 warp yarns, stripped

Analysis by Walter B. Denny and Sumru Belger Krody

11
LARGE-PATTERN HOLBEIN CARPET

Probably central Anatolia, probably 17th century
The Textile Museum R34.2.1
Acquired by George Hewitt Myers in 1928
178 × 108 cm (70 × 42 1/2 in)

Large-pattern Holbein carpets are named after a carpet depicted in Hans Holbein the Younger's double portrait of the French ambassadors in the National Gallery, London (1533). This style of carpet is rare in Western collections, and only two classical examples are found in the United States: this example and one in Philadelphia Museum of Art (Ellis 1988, no. 2). The earliest example known, conceivably from the late 13th century, is in the Vakıflar Museum in Istanbul (Balpınar and Hirsch 1988, no. 1), and the earliest example in a Western collection is found in the Museum für Islamische Kunst, Berlin (Spuhler 1987, pl. 4). Early examples of the same design, in totally different weave structures, are found in two surviving "para-Mamluk" carpets that we attribute to Tabriz (Ellis 1988, no. 1; Spuhler 1988, pl. 74), and in one unpublished silk-pile carpet thought to be from Timurid Iran, perhaps Herat, now in a Persian Gulf collection. A further testimony to the popularity of the design is found in a number of early Spanish carpets with the same design, including two in The Textile Museum (R44.2.7 and R44.00.5) and one in the Cleveland Museum of Art (1952.511). Carpets of this group are thought to be the "wheel" carpets mentioned in a number of early European inventories (Pinner 1986).

This carpet from The Textile Museum collections shows three of the large octagonal motifs that define the type. Each is in a rectangular compartment whose proportions indicate a vertical compression of the design. Four triangular cornerpieces fill out the three compartments, which are surrounded by a stylized vine with blossoms. The main border of white on red contains a late version of the kufesque border found in early examples. The colors of this example are unusual, and it is possible that prolonged exposure to light has altered them from their original hues.

Published: Mackie 1974, no. 28

WARP: wool: off-white (undyed), 2 Z-spun yarns plied S; alternate warps slightly depressed

WEFT: wool: light pink-orange wool, 1 Z-spun yarn; 2 shoots

PILE: wool: dark red, pink-orange, green varying in shade to yellow (abrash), dark yellow, dark blue varying in shade to light blue (abrash), off-white (undyed), black-brown (corroded), 2 Z-spun yarns plied S

symmetrical knot, V 28 × H 22 per dm (7 × 5 1/2 per in)

EDGES: flat selvedge of 4 warp yarns woven in pink-orange weft

ENDS: stripped

Analysis by Charles Grant Ellis and Walter B. Denny

12
LARGE-PATTERN HOLBEIN CARPET

Probably north-central Anatolia, 18th or 19th century
Anonymous Collector, Pennsylvania
219 × 173 cm (86 × 68 in)

This carpet is a testimony to the survival of the designs of the classical large-pattern Holbein carpets into later centuries. The traces of the strapwork in the octagonal medallions are clearly seen, both as a blue arabesque and as a series of tiny white diamond shapes. The cornerpieces around each medallion likewise reflect the design of 15th-century prototypes.

The two small triangular ornaments, with three pendants to either side of the bottom, octagon are of special interest. They are depictions of jewelry that were added by the weaver as *nazarlık*, ornaments intended to ward off the evil eye of jealous spirits (see also cat. no. 43).

The distinctive border of this rug is shared by a group of carpets with varying field designs, many of them reflecting different kinds of classical prototypes. Some of the most exciting examples are now in Istanbul museums (Balpınar and Hirsch 1988, nos. 14–16; Ölçer, Enderlein, Batári, and Mills 1996, pls. 39–44).

The top and bottom of this carpet are easy to determine from the design. Starting expansively, the weaver was forced to crowd the second octagon and its attendant ornaments into a smaller space than the first in order to finish the carpet before she ran out of warp yarns. At the same time, the small pendant jewelry ornaments, hanging from the triangular motifs, clearly show the weaving direction.

WARP: wool; off-white (undyed), 2 Z-spun yarns plied S; one level

WEFT: wool; red, 1 Z-spun yarn; 2–4 shoots, occasionally 3 (2// + 1) shoots

PILE: wool; red, dark orange, pink-orange, blue varying in shade (*abrash*), blue-green, purple, yellow, off-white (undyed), black-brown, 2 Z-spun yarns plied S

symmetrical knot, V 36 × H 28 per dm
(9 × 7 per in)

EDGES: cut, reselvedged

ENDS: extensively rewoven, but the row of pile ornaments, on the tapestry-weave bands at each end, appears to reflect the original design

Analysis by Walter B. Denny and Sumru Belger Krody

13
LARGE-PATTERN HOLBEIN
YASTIK FACE

Probably central Anatolia, 19th century
Collection of Jon M. and Deborah Anderson
101 × 61 cm (40 × 24 in)

So powerful and popular was the influence of
the classical large-pattern Holbein prototypes
that they were reproduced in many different
sizes, including small cushion covers such as
this 19th-century example. The rich, slightly
corroded, purple-brown pile and distinctive
selvedge may localize this *yastik* face to the
Karapınar district in Konya province.

WARP: wool: off-white (undyed), 2 Z-spun yarns
plied S; one level; coarse wool does not hold its
spin where stripped

WEFT: wool: off-white (undyed), some brown
(undyed), 1 Z-spun yarn of varying thickness; 2–4
shoots, some instances of 4 (2// + 2//) shoots

PILE: wool: red, yellow, purple-brown (corroded),
black-brown (corroded), off-white (undyed), light
purple faded to gray-brown, 2 Z-spun yarns
plied S

symmetrical knot, V 30–34 × H 25–26 per dm
(8–9 × 6–7 per in)

EDGES: flat selvedge of 4 bundles of 2 warp yarns,
wrapped in dark purple-brown wool

ENDS: stripped

Analysis by Walter B. Denny and
Sumru Belger Krody

14
MEMLING-PATTERN *YASTIK*-SIZED RUG

Probably eastern Anatolia, 19th century
Collection of Jon M. and Deborah Anderson
64 × 44 cm (25 1/2 × 17 1/2 in)

In size, this small rug resembles a *yastık* or cushion cover, but its design suggests it may also have been woven as a sampler for a large yellow-ground carpet, probably a long runner. The use of a loosely packed, irregular, and often heavy weft is responsible for areas of vertical stretching of the design.

The "Memling" *gül*, or small repeating geometric medallion motif, is seen here characteristically encompassed within an octagon. It takes its name from the depiction of a similar motif in a sumak depicted in a still-life painting by Hans Memling. The motif is seen to better advantage in catalogue number 15, a larger rug using the same motif.

The use of a yellow ground and the secondary motif of small multicolored squares are found in many rugs with this design, irrespective of their weave structure and provenance, although such carpets are frequently attributed to Konya province (Kirchheim, Franses, Spuhler, Muse, Rageth, and Hermann 1993, pp. 186–198). Many examples of early Memling carpets are seen in European paintings, but only two classical examples thought to be from the 15th or 16th century have survived; one, with staggered rows of *gül* forms on a white ground, is in the Museum of Applied Arts, Budapest (No. 14.427; see Batári 1994, p. 96; Ölçer, Enderlein, Batári, and Mills 1996, pl. 58). The other, with stacked rows on a yellow ground, is in the Mevlana Museum in Konya (No. 859; see Ölçer, Enderlein, Batári, and Mills 1996, pl. 56).

WARP: wool: off-white (undyed), 2 Z-spun yarns plied S; one level, looped at bottom end; warp yarn tends to lose spin and twist where stripped

WEFT: wool: off-white (undyed) or very light brown, 1 Z-spun yarn; 2–4 shoots, mostly 3 (occasionally 2// + 1) shoots

PILE: wool: yellow, red, orange-pink, purple (faded), blue, black-brown (corroded), white (undyed), 2 Z-spun yarns plied S

symmetrical knot pulled to the right,
V 18 × H 21 per dm (4 1/2 × 5 per in)

EDGES: bundle of 4 warp yarns wrapped in very light brown weft wool on each side

ENDS: bottom: 5 cm loose very light-brown tapestry weave, with the last three shoots before the looped ends consisting of orange pile wool; top: approximately 2.5 cm very light-brown tapestry weave, stripped

Analysis by Walter B. Denny and Sumru Belger Krody

15
MEMLING-PATTERN CARPET

Central Anatolia, probably 19th century
Collection of Jon M. and Deborah Anderson
175 × 117 cm (69 × 46 in)

The popularity of the "Memling" *gül* in certain parts of Anatolia resulted in the weaving of a large group of yellow-ground carpets that have been frequently seen in print in recent years. The motif is historically related to a specific Türkmen tribal group, although the identity of that group is not presently known. The appearance in certain Türkmen weavings from Central Asia establishes strong links with the Turkic nomadic past.

WARP: wool: very light brown (undyed), some dark-brown (undyed), 2 Z-spun yarns plied S; one level

WEFT: wool: light red-brown, 1 Z-spun yarn; 2–6 shoots

PILE: wool: light purple, dark purple, red, blue, orange, yellow varying in shade (*abrash*), green varying in shade (*abrash*), black-brown (uncorroded and possibly undyed) wool

symmetrical knot, V 22–23 × H 20 per dm (6 × 5 per in)

EDGES: flat selvedge covered with light-reddish brown weft, outside bundle of 4 warp yarns, then 3 bundles of 2 warp yarns

ENDS: warp yarns gathered together in bunches of 2–4, mostly 4, then knotted

Analysis by Walter B. Denny and Sumru Belger Krody

16
HOLBEIN-VARIANT
PATTERN CARPET

Central Anatolia, possibly Konya province,
probably 16th or 17th century
Marshall and Marilyn R. Wolf Collection
178 × 155 cm (70 × 61 in)

The diamond-shaped motifs on this
fragmentary carpet belong to a well-defined
group of early Anatolian carpets, which
appear to incorporate elements both of the
"Holbein" family and the "Ghirlandaio"
family of designs (cat. nos. 17–19). Between
the earliest production of the design in the
15th century and a late revival of the design in
large commercially woven sumaks, produced
in the late 19th century in Transcaucasia,
there are very few surviving examples such as
this to indicate continuing use of the design
over the centuries. The red-and-white border
on this carpet, while preserving the
traditional colors used in such kufesque
borders over many centuries, shows an
attractive disposition of motifs at a very far-
removed form from the original.

WARP: wool: very light brown or off-white (undyed),
2 Z-spun yarns plied S; one level

WEFT: wool: dark red, 1 Z-spun yarn; 2–4 shoots

PILE: wool: red, blue, green, yellow, white (undyed),
purple, black-brown (corroded), 2 Z-spun yarns
plied S

symmetrical knot, V 30 × H 26 per dm
(7 1/2 × 6 1/2 per in)

EDGES: cut

ENDS: cut

Analysis by Walter B. Denny and
Sumru Belger Krody

17
GHIRLANDAIO-PATTERN CARPET

Western or northwestern Anatolia, probably 18th or 19th century

The Textile Museum 1997.9.1

Gift of Mrs. Elbert Mathews

180 × 145 cm (71 × 57 in)

Named after Domenico Ghirlandaio, the "Ghirlandaio" carpets, like the "Memlings" and "Holbeins," exhibit geometric designs with extensive use of interwoven white stripes (strapwork) to define motifs and borders. The characteristic medallion appears in one rare instance in staggered rows as a field pattern, in a beautiful carpet in the Museum für Islamische Kunst, Berlin (Spuhler 1988, pl. 19).

The major motifs of this carpet are composed of motifs from large-pattern Holbein prototypes that have been reassembled. The antecedents of the octagon in the center of each motif are clear enough; the triangular motifs projecting from each side of the square are adapted from the spandrels or cornerpieces found in the large-pattern Holbein carpets (cat. no. 12).

Two similar but earlier carpets in this design were given by Joseph V. McMullan to The Metropolitan Museum of Art (McMullan 1965, pls. 97 and 98). The green ground of this example may have been dyed with one of the earliest "synthetic" dyes, a chemically treated form of indigo.

WARP: wool: white (undyed), 2 Z-spun yarns plied S; one level

WEFT: wool: red, 1 Z-spun yarn; 2–3 shoots

PILE: wool: red, blue, yellow, light green (faded), pink-orange, light purple (faded), white (undyed), black-brown (corroded), 2 Z-spun yarns plied S

symmetrical knot, V 27–28 × H 24–25 per dm (7 × 6 per in)

EDGES: flat selvedge, outer bundle of 2 warp yarns, then 2 individual warp yarns, wrapped in red weft wool

ENDS: bottom: stripped, bound; top: 1 cm red tapestry weave, stripped

Analysis by Walter B. Denny and Sumru Belger Krody

18

GHIRLANDAIO-PATTERN CARPET

Western or northwestern Anatolia, probably 18th or 19th century

The Textile Museum R34.2.8

Acquired by George Hewitt Myers in 1913

216 × 137 cm (85 × 54 in)

With a design inspired by a variety of sources, from the border taken from the 19th-century Ladik rugs, to the red-blue palette taken from Ushak carpets, and to the "Ghirlandaio" medallion in the center, this carpet shows the ability of Anatolian weavers to create new compositions by assembling classical motifs.

WARP: wool: off-white (undyed), 2 Z-spun yarns plied S; one level

WEFT: wool: red, 1 Z-spun yarn; 3–7 shoots, some instances of 3 (2// + 1) shoots

PILE: wool: red, yellow, blue, black-brown (slightly corroded), light brown (corroded), off-white (undyed), green, dark red-purple, 2 Z-spun yarns plied S

symmetrical knot, V 22–24 × H 24–26 per dm (5–6 × 6–7 per in)

EDGES: flat selvedge wrapped in red weft, 2 outer bundles of 2 warp yarns, 2 inner individual warp yarns

ENDS: stripped

Analysis by Walter B. Denny and Sumru Belger Krody

19
GHIRLANDAIO- AND BELLINI-PATTERN CARPET

Probably east-central or eastern Anatolia,
18th century

Anonymous Collector, Pennsylvania

198 × 142 cm (78 × 56 in)

The central motif of this carpet is yet another
variant on the Ghirlandaio pattern, while the
ends reflect an entirely different group of
carpets known as "Bellini" carpets. The
meaning of the octagonal compartment,
formed by a border that intrudes in the main
field of the carpet, has been hotly debated.
Some see it as a stylized mountain adapted
from Chinese prototypes, while others prefer
to see in it the representation of a classical
Islamic fountain. By the time this carpet was
woven, these origins were far-removed in
time and meaning from the village weaver.

Carpets such as this, although almost
certainly woven in Anatolia, provided the
inspiration for a type of late 19th-century
Transcaucasian carpet woven in the Kuba
area; a testament to the continuing diffusion
of classical Anatolian designs.

WARP: wool: white (undyed), some off-white
(undyed) and brown (undyed) wool yarns plied
together, yarn irregular in material and thickness,
2 Z-spun yarns plied S; one level

WEFT: wool: red and dark red, 1 Z-spun yarn;
2–4 shoots, 3 shoots (2//+1)

PILE: wool: red, blue varying in shade (*abrash*),
dark green, light yellow, off-white (undyed), black-
brown (corroded), 2 Z-spun yarns plied S

symmetrical knot, V 28–31 × H 24–27 per dm
(7–8 × 6–7 per in)

EDGES: flat selvedge, red weft over 4 bundles of
2 warp yarns

ENDS: bottom: 7 cm red tapestry weave with
light-green bands; top: stripped

Analysis Walter B. Denny and
Sumru Belger Krody

20

OTTOMAN COURT CARPET FRAGMENT

Istanbul or Bursa, late 16th century
The Textile Museum R34.33.5
Acquired by George Hewitt Myers in 1918
164 × 122 cm (64 × 48 in)

The quatrefoil (four-lobed) medallion, defined by split-leaf motifs and seen here in white, is one of the most pervasive of all Anatolian carpet motifs from the classical age. It consists of a four-lobed medallion, with each lobe containing either a lotus blossom or a more complex lotus palmette. It appears early on, in the secondary motifs of the small-pattern Holbein carpets from the 14th century onward (cat. nos. 5–8); in Ushak medallion carpets from the 15th and 16th centuries; and then reappears in many different incarnations in Anatolian weaving through the 20th century. It is also abstracted in the so-called *shemle-gül* motif of certain old Türkmen carpets from Central Asia. The form may stem from architectural decoration, but its exact origins and meaning remain an object of speculation.

Published: Kühnel and Bellinger 1957, p. 63

WARP: silk: off-white (undyed), 2 and 3 Z-twisted yarns plied S; alternate warps depressed

WEFT: silk: dark red, untwisted (too lightly twisted for analysis); 2 shoots; occasional red or blue discontinuous wefts of 2 Z-twisted S plied yarns used as "shims"

PILE: wool: light blue, dark blue, dark red, yellow, yellow-green, dark blue-green, orange, black-brown, mostly 2 Z-spun yarns plied S; cotton: white (undyed), 2 S-spun yarns plied Z

asymmetrical knot open left, V 41–42 × H 59 per dm (10–11 × 15 per in)

EDGES: cut

ENDS: cut, stripped

CONSTRUCTION: 5 fragments sewn together

Analysis by Charles Grant Ellis and Walter B. Denny

21
CARPET FRAGMENT WITH QUATREFOIL PATTERN IN HEXAGONAL LOZENGES AND BORDER FRAGMENT

Probably central or east-central Anatolia, 17th or 18th century

Collection of Marshall and Marilyn R. Wolf

Main field fragment: 121 × 114 cm (47 ¹/₂ × 45 in)

Border fragment: 27 × 140 cm (10 ¹/₂ × 55 in)

Here a simplified form of the quatrefoil, with the flowers in each compartment clearly visible, is contained in hexagonal compartments. The restricted palette of this carpet is unusual, perhaps indicating that the field design had a prototype in woven silk textiles.

WARP: wool: white (undyed), coarse, 2 Z-spun yarns plied S; one level

WEFT: wool: red, 1 Z-spun yarn; 4–6 alternate shoots

PILE: wool: red, blue varying in shade (*abrash*), yellow, white (undyed), black-brown (uncorroded), yellow (only in the main field fragment), 2 Z-spun yarns plied S

symmetrical knot, V 25–26 × H 25–27 per dm (6–7 × 6–8 per in)

EDGES: cut

ENDS: cut, stripped

Analysis by Walter B. Denny and Sumru Belger Krody

SMALL CARPET WITH CENTRAL QUATREFOIL MEDALLION

Western Anatolia, probably Ushak, late 16th century

Anonymous Collector, Pennsylvania

157 × 102 cm (62 × 40 in)

Erroneously termed "double-ended prayer rugs," these small quatrefoil medallion carpets are thought to have been woven in Ushak. With their cloud-band borders and complex cornerpieces, they are probably among the earliest carpets to utilize this now familiar medallion format. Upon close examination, each cornerpiece is actually a quarter of a large, elaborate, and deeply indented medallion, but there is little in either end of this carpet that suggests an arch. The single motif at the top of the carpet is an enigma. It certainly does not represent a lamp, nor any ornament commonly found in mosques, which serves as a *nazarlık* or charm against evil spirits. Nevertheless, by breaking the symmetry of the rug and thereby "marring" a "perfection" that might have drawn the envy of the evil eye, this motif may indeed serve precisely that function.

Published: Christie's London, 1996, lot 411; Hali, 1997, p. 120

WARP: wool: off-white (undyed), 2 Z-spun yarns plied S; alternate warps slightly depressed; warp retains its spin or twist where stripped

WEFT: wool: red, 1 Z-spun yarn; 2 shoots or 3 (2// + 1) shoots; discontinuous wefts cause pattern of diagonals (lazy lines) on back of carpet

PILE: wool: red, pink, dark blue, green varying in shade (*abrash*), yellow, light yellow-orange, black-brown, white (undyed), 2 Z-spun yarns plied S

symmetrical knot, V 49–56 × H 34 per dm (13–14 × 8 1/2 –9 per in)

EDGES: restored, reselvedged

ENDS: both have less than 1 cm of tapestry weave banded green (outer) and red (inner)

Analysis by Walter B. Denny and Sumru Belger Krody

23

SMALL CARPET WITH CENTRAL QUATREFOIL MEDALLION

Probably central Anatolia, 18th or 19th century
From a Massachusetts Collector
185 × 130 cm (73 × 51 in)

A triumph of color, this small carpet also displays a design that is amazingly complex. The coloration of the central quatrefoil medallion—red, yellow, and blue—suggests it was inspired by a commercial carpet from Ushak. This carpet shows the weaver's debt to the past, but in the rest of its design the carpet demonstrates a fresh and powerful originality.

Published: Hali, 1996, p. 140

WARP: wool: white (undyed), 2 Z-spun yarns plied S; one level

WEFT: wool: red, 1 Z-spun yarn; mostly 2 shoots

PILE: wool: purple, yellow, light red, dark red, blue, green, black-brown (slightly corroded), off-white (undyed), 2 Z-spun yarns plied S

symmetrical knot, V 35–36 × H 25–26 per dm
(9 × 6$^1/_2$ per in)

EDGES: fragments of original edges remain, flat selvedge, four bundles of 1, 2, 2, and 2 warp yarns respectively from outside in, wrapped with red weft

ENDS: bottom: fragments of original red tapestry weave; top: stripped

Analysis by Walter B. Denny

24
LOTTO-PATTERN CARPET FRAGMENT

Probably central Anatolia, early 17th century
The Textile Museum R34.18.4
Acquired by George Hewitt Myers in 1928
160 × 137 cm (63 × 54 in)

A carpet quite similar to this example, evidently either new or in an excellent state of preservation, was depicted by the Dutch painter G. Van Honthorst (1590–1656) in his painting *De vrolijke speelman* (known in English as *The Merry Fiddler*) in the Rijksmuseum, Amsterdam. The end finish of the very carefully portrayed carpet in the painting, consists of what appears to be about 6 cm of dark-green tapestry weave and a fringe of red warp yarns about 14 cm in length. This suggests that in some cases the fringes of Lotto carpets exported to Europe may have been dyed red to enhance their marketability.

Published: Mackie 1974, no. 31

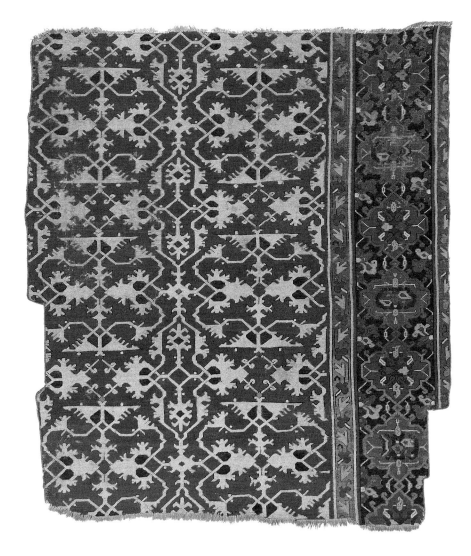

WARP: wool: off-white (undyed), 2 Z-spun yarns plied S; alternate warps slightly depressed

WEFTS: wool: light red, 1 Z-spun yarn; 2 shoots

PILE: wool: orange-red, dark brown-red, dark blue, light blue, dark green, light green, yellow, light orange, off-white (undyed), black-brown, 2 Z-spun yarns plied S

symmetrical knot, V 34 × H 26 per dm
(8$^1/_2$ –9 × 6$^1/_2$ –7 per in)

EDGES: cut

ENDS: cut

Analysis by Charles Grant Ellis and Walter B. Denny

25
LOTTO-PATTERN CARPET FRAGMENT

Probably central Anatolia, early 17th century
Marshall and Marilyn R. Wolf Collection
142 × 119 (56 × 47 in)

As Charles Grant Ellis noted, carpets with the Lotto pattern were woven in several different places over an extended period of time, from the early 16th century through the late 18th century (Ellis 1975). Judging from the number surviving in European collections and depicted in European paintings, they were highly popular in Europe. The earliest carpets using the familiar yellow arabesque on red ground are apparently large examples from the early 16th century, with what we have called "calligraphic" kufesque borders. By the 17th century, borders with small medallion-like forms such as this one, were more commonly found.

If we analyze the yellow arabesque carefully, we can see that it is composed of two elements: a smaller quatrefoil or cruciform motif and a larger, roughly octagonal motif. Both of these motifs are directly derived from a Timurid *rumi* arabesque prototype. The simplification and geometrization that occurred early on in the carpet medium—in the classical examples of the early 16th century—created one of the most popular carpet designs of all time. With very few basic changes, these motifs continued to inspire Anatolian weavers for centuries, and were copied as far afield as Spain in the 17th century.

WARP: wool: off-white (undyed), 2 Z-spun yarns plied S; alternate warps slightly depressed
WEFT: wool: light red, 1 Z-spun yarn; 2 shoots
PILE: wool: orange-red, dark brown-red, dark blue, light blue, green, yellow, light orange, dark purple, off-white (undyed), black-brown, 2 Z-spun yarns plied S
symmetrical knot, V 33–34 × H 26–27 per dm
(8 × 7 per in)
EDGES: cut
ENDS: cut

Analysis by Walter B. Denny and
Sumru Belger Krody

26

SMALL LOTTO-PATTERN CARPET

Central or east-central Anatolia, 17th or
18th century
Anonymous Collector, Pennsylvania
149 × 125 cm (58 1/2 × 49 in)

Carpets with the popular Lotto pattern
rarely depart from the scheme of a yellow
arabesque on a red ground, but the present
example shows the familiar pattern in blue
upon red. The brown-ground "ragged leaf"
border of this carpet is quite distinctive.
A group of central or east-central Anatolian
rugs—many of them in *sajjadah* size such
as this—with various field designs, share
a common technique and border design.
It has been noted that such borders almost
always show their deeply serrated forms
facing alternately in and out, rather than
stacked vertically as in this example.

Published: Christie's London 2001, lot 117

WARP: wool: off-white (undyed), 2 Z-spun yarns
plied S; alternate warps slightly depressed

WEFTS: wool: red wool, 1 Z-spun yarn; 2, 3 (2// + 1)
and 4 (2// + 2//) shoots, loosely packed

PILE: wool: red, light red, yellow, blue, blue-green
varying in shade (*abrash*), off-white (undyed),
black-brown (corroded), 2 Z-spun yarns plied S

symmetrical knot, V 42–48 × H 31–32 per dm
(11–12 × 8 per in)

EDGES: restored, rewoven

ENDS: restored, rewoven

Analysis: Walter B. Denny and
Sumru Belger Krody

27
CARPET FRAGMENT

Probably central or east-central Anatolia, possibly
16th century or earlier
From a Massachusetts Collector
99 × 144 cm (39 × 56¹/₂ in)

This remarkable rug, with its unusual color range, design, and complete absence of white wool in the design, is clearly modeled after a silk textile with a pattern of flower-filled ogival compartments, defined by a medium-blue vine with *rumi* split-leaf forms. The majority of Turkish carpets, modeled after ogival-pattern silk textiles, use Ottoman models from the mid-16th century or later. This carpet is probably patterned after a 15th-century silk textile—Ottoman, Mamluk, or most likely Timurid—where the use of the *rumi* motif in a lattice was more common.

Published: Sotheby's New York 1993, lot 80

WARP: wool: off-white (undyed), some light-brown and off-white (undyed) wool yarn plied together, 2 Z-spun yarns plied S; one level

WEFT: wool: red, brown (possibly undyed), 1 Z-spun yarn; 2 shoots, loosely packed

PILE: wool: light brown varying in shade (*abrash*), medium blue, light red, dark red, dark green, light green, light purple, light orange, dark yellow, black-brown (corroded), 2 and occasionally 3 Z-spun yarns plied S

symmetrical knot, V 33–34 × H 25–26 per dm (8¹/₂ × 6¹/₂ per in)

EDGES: small fragment of flat selvedge on right side shows red weft over 6 pairs of warp yarns

ENDS: cut

NOTE: bottom (beginning of weaving) of carpet is at top of illustration

Analysis by Walter B. Denny

28
CARPET WITH OGIVAL DESIGN

Probably western Anatolia, 18th or 19th century
Marshall and Marilyn R. Wolf Collection
290 × 168 cm (114 × 66 in)

The typical western Anatolian construction of
this rug does not prepare one for the shock
of its rather intense colors, especially the
yellow, and the unusually bold and large-scale
pattern. This carpet may well trace the origin
of its motifs to the same 15th-century group
of prototypes as catalogue number 27.

WARP: wool; off-white (undyed), 2 Z-spun yarns
plied S; one level

WEFT: wool: light pink, 1 Z-spun yarn; 2–4 shoots,
mostly 4 shoots

PILE: wool: dark blue, green, red, yellow, white
(undyed), black-brown, 2 Z-spun yarns plied S

symmetrical knot, V 28 × H 22 per dm
(7 × 5 1/2 per in)

EDGES: flat selvedge, 4 bundles of 2 warp yarns
wrapped in red pile yarn

ENDS: bottom: 12–13 cm red tapestry weave,
1 cm flat transverse braid, braided warp ends; top:
11–12 cm red tapestry weave, 1 cm flat transverse
braid, braided warp ends

Analysis by Walter B. Denny and
Sumru Belger Krody

29
CARPET WITH OGIVAL LATTICE DESIGN

Probably south-central Anatolia, 17th or
18th century
The Textile Museum R34.12.6
Acquired by George Hewitt Myers in 1913
216 × 165 cm (86 × 65 in)

This carpet, with its variant kufesque border,
blue-green ground, dense weave, and ogival
lattice design is a splendid work of art. The
small-scale ogival lattice of vines and leaves
suggests a 15th-century design ancestry
similar to those of catalogue numbers 27 and
28. Here, however, the design is on a much
smaller scale, probably much closer in spirit
to the silk textiles that inspired it.

Published: Mackie 1974, no. 44

WARP: wool: off-white (undyed), 2 Z-spun yarns
plied S; one level, some warp yarns lose twist
where stripped

WEFT: wool: red, 1 fine Z-spun yarn; 2–4 shoots

PILE: wool: blue, green, yellow, red, purple, white
(undyed), black-brown, 2 Z-spun yarns plied S

symmetrical knot, V 37 × H 29–30 per dm
(9$^1/_2$ × 7$^1/_2$ per in)

EDGES: restored

ENDS: bottom: reconstructed; top: stripped

Analysis by Walter B. Denny and
Sumru Belger Krody

30
YASTIK FACE

Western or northwestern Anatolia, mid- to late
19th century
Collection of Jon M. and Deborah Anderson
95–96 × 56 cm (37¹/₂ × 22 in)

Probably woven at least 200 years after the
prototype (cat. no. 29), this little cushion
cover exemplifies the often startling manner
in which Anatolian village weavers took
elements of overall repeat patterns and
radically adapted them to different formats,
colors, and weave structures.

WARP: wool: off-white (undyed), 2 Z-spun yarns
plied S; one level; relatively soft warp holds spin
and twist well where stripped

WEFT: wool: off-white (undyed), some medium
brown (possibly undyed), 1 Z-spun yarn; 2 shoots

PILE: wool; red, yellow, green, blue, very light brown
(possibly faded purple), light brown, off-white
(undyed), black-brown, 2 Z-spun yarns plied S

symmetrical knot, V 32 × H 28–29 per dm
(8 × 7 per in)

EDGES: flat selvedge of a pair of outer warp yarns
plus 5 single warp yarns, wrapped in varicolored
pile wool

ENDS: bottom: 6–7 cm red-and-blue tapestry
weave with row of small pile ornaments; top: 6 cm
red and green tapestry weave with row of small-
pile ornaments

Analysis by Walter B. Denny and
Sumru Belger Krody

31
YASTIK FACE

Probably northeast Anatolia, late 19th century
Collection of Jon M. and Deborah Anderson
91–92 × 66 cm (36 × 26 in)

With its use of three-ply warps and wefts
more characteristic of south-Transcaucasian
carpets, unusual coloration, and its design
inspiration in a white-ground Transcaucasian
embroidery, this *yastık* face probably comes
from the northeastern corner of Anatolia.

In it we see yet another example of the
remarkable inclination of Anatolian pile
carpet weavers to absorb designs from other
textile media. In this case, the weavers were
inspired by a group of silk-embroidered
textiles on white-cotton ground, thought to
have originated in the eastern part of
Transcaucasia, with vertical strings of five-
petalled lotus blossoms and small octagons
ornamented with swastika-like "pinwheel"
motifs.

WARP: wool: pinkish, very light brown, 3 Z-spun
yarns plied S; alternate warps slightly depressed

WEFT: wool: very light brown or darkened off-white
(undyed), 2 or 3 Z-spun yarns plied S; 2 shoots

PILE: wool: dark blue, light blue, blue green, yellow,
red, purple (slightly corroded), medium brown
(probably undyed), off-white (undyed), 2 Z-spun
yarns plied S

symmetrical knot, V 27–33 × H 30–31 per dm
(7–8 1/2 × 7 1/2 per in)

EDGES: 2 bundles of 2 warp yarns wrapped in
red pile yarn

ENDS: stripped

Analysis by Walter B. Denny and
Sumru Belger Krody

32
YASTIK FACE

Probably central Anatolia, early 19th century
From a Massachusetts Collector
97 × 60 cm (38 × 23 1/2 in)

The design of this handsome and colorful
yastık face, typical of a group of central
Anatolian cushion-cover rugs from various
provenances, is adapted quite literally
from a type of voided velvet *yastık*, woven in
17th-century Bursa (cat. no. 33). However, the
weaver has chosen brilliant colors and
accommodated the design to the limitations
of the pile technique by simplifying certain
motifs. The group of cushion covers to which
this particular rug belongs is distinguished by
the very sparing use of black-brown outlines.
Here it appears only in the highly geometric
cornerpieces of the field.

WARP: wool: off-white (undyed), 2 Z-spun yarns
plied S; one level

WEFT: wool: dark brown (probably undyed),
1 Z-spun yarn; 2, 4 (2// + 2//) shoots

PILE: wool: red, yellow, green, blue, purple, white
(undyed), black-brown (slightly corroded),
2 Z-spun yarns plied S

symmetrical knot, V 20–21 × H 20–21 per dm
(5 × 5 per in)

EDGES: 2 bundles of 2 warp yarns wrapped in
dark purple pile wool

ENDS: stripped

Analysis by Walter B. Denny

33
YASTIK FACE

Bursa, probably 17th century or later
The Textile Museum 1.79
Gift of Mrs. Hoffman Philip
129 × 67 cm (50 × 26 in)

Woven with dark-red and light-green silk, this
voided velvet *yastık* face, was probably one
of a pair or quartet. It was destined to rest
on a bench-sofa built against the wall of an
Ottoman room. The central medallion is
ornamented with eight peacock-feather
motifs, the two pendants are decorated at
the ends with five hyacinth blossoms each;
four sprigs of three leaves help to fill out the
crimson field. The cornerpieces are adorned
with two-blossom, dark-red sprays, and the
six compartments (lappets) of each end
panel bear a design of a large and complex
rosebud. All of these floral forms originated
in Ottoman court art after the middle of the
16th century, the invention of the artist-
designer Kara Memi and his followers. The
repertoire of stylized garden flowers has
come to define much of Ottoman court
art since that time.

WARPS: main: silk: off-white, slightly S-twisted;
pile: silk: dark red, pink (faded), green, slightly
S-twisted

WEFTS: silk: off-white, no-twist; cotton: off-white,
Z-spun; supplementary: metallic-wrapped silk
thread: metal strips Z-twisted around off-white
silk core thread

EDGES: selvedge

ENDS: cut

34
STAR USHAK CARPET

West-central Anatolia, late 16th century
The Textile Museum R34.1.1
Acquired by George Hewitt Myers in 1918
308 × 185 cm (121 × 72 1/2 in)

Woven in large sizes in the characteristic
color palette of Ushak, in which red, dark
blue, and yellow predominate, the "star"
Ushak carpets, with their deeply indented
octofoil medallions and diamond-shaped
secondary motifs, are probably among the
earliest types of commercial weaving
produced by the Ushak manufactories
from the late 15th century onward. The
design is clearly related to the 15th-century
tilework of Azerbaijan and Anatolia, using
rumi ornaments in the blue-ground star
medallions, and an arabesque of vines
and lotus blossoms in the field. The rather
pronounced vertical compacting of weft
and pile yarns affect the appearance of the
medallions in this carpet. This characteristic
probably places it later rather than earlier
in the chronology of such Ushak carpets.
Earlier examples, such as the McMullan
carpet in The Metropolitan Museum of Art
(McMullan 1965, no. 67), usually show a
more 1:1 knot ratio.

WARP: wool: off-white (undyed), 2 Z-spun yarns
plied S, some dark brown (undyed) yarn plied with
off-white (undyed) yarn; alternate warps depressed

WEFT: wool: light red, 1 Z-spun yarn; 2 shoots;
discontinuous wefts cause pattern of diagonals
(lazy lines) on back of rug

PILE: wool: dark red, light blue varying in shade
(*abrash*), dark blue, yellow-green, yellow, orange,
off-white (undyed), black-brown (corroded),
2 Z-spun yarns plied S

symmetrical knot, V 26–27 × H 16–17
(6 1/2 × 4 per in)

EDGES: cut

ENDS: cut

Analysis by Charles Grant Ellis and Walter B. Denny

35
SMALL USHAK MEDALLION CARPET

Western Anatolia, late 18th century
Anonymous Collector, Pennsylvania
195 × 112 cm (76^1/$_2$ × 44 in)

The medallion carpets of Ushak—with their characteristic red, blue, and yellow coloration, *rumi*-decorated ogival medallions, surrounded by a deeply serrated "collar", with pendants at each end and one-color leaf arabesque, usually blue on a red ground—were produced in western Anatolia for well over 300 years, evidently beginning in the later 15th century (Raby 1986b). Produced in a number of different weaving centers and ateliers in a range of sizes, with many different design and color variations, the majority are quite large (Lanier 1975, nos. 28–33; Ölçer and Denny 1999, pls. 52–64). Small examples of any age are quite rare (Ölçer and Denny 1999, pl. 63). This exceptionally small and late example represents the type and tradition. The classic commercial rugs of Ushak, from the 16th and 17th centuries, spawned a remarkable lineage in subsequent Anatolian weaving (cat. nos. 37–39). The complex designs of the medallion carpets, which are very difficult to render in village and nomadic weavings, are mostly confined to the products of Ushak itself, even in much later weavings—as in this example.

WARP: wool; white (undyed), 2 Z-spun yarns plied S; one level

WEFT: wool: red, 1 Z-spun yarn; mostly 2 shoots, rarely 3 (alternate or 2// + 1) shoots; discontinuous wefts cause pattern of diagonals (lazy lines) on back of rug

PILE: wool: dark red, light red, light blue, dark blue-green, yellow, black-brown; 2 Z-spun yarns plied S

symmetrical knot, V 31 × H 28–29 per dm (8 × 7 per in)

EDGES: restored

ENDS: restored

Analysis by Walter B. Denny and Sumru Belger Krody

38
EIGHT-LOBED MEDALLION
USHAK CARPET

Western Anatolia, 16th century
Marshall and Marilyn R. Wolf Collection
262 × 153 cm (103 × 60 in)

One of the most handsome types of Ushak
carpet uses an eight-lobed medallion and
a wider variety of cooler colors—blues and
greens—than is usually seen in Ushak
carpets. Clearly the product of a particular
specialized atelier within the large complex
of weaving establishments in the Ushak
district, this carpet and others like it show
medallions with parallels in the weaving of
northwestern Iran.

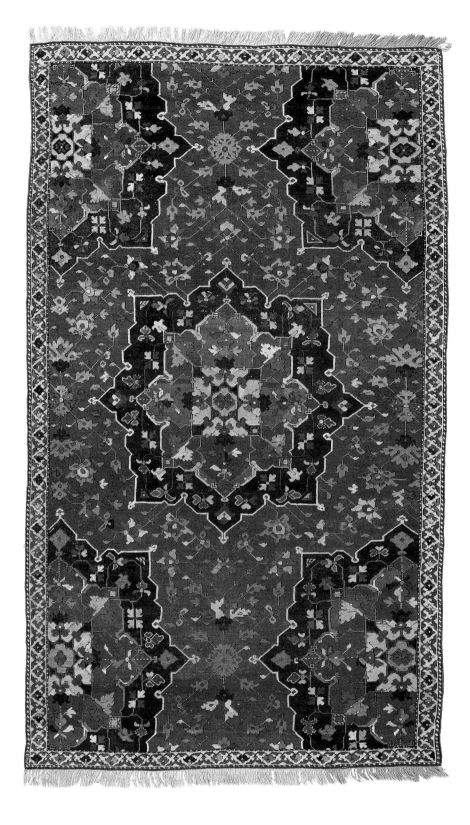

WARP: wool: off-white (undyed), 2 Z-spun yarns
plied S; alternate warps slightly depressed

WEFT: wool: red, 1 Z-spun yarn; 2 shoots;
discontinuous wefts cause pattern of diagonals
(lazy lines) on back of rug

PILE: wool: light blue, medium blue, dark blue,
dark red, light red, light green (slightly corroded),
medium green, dark green, dark yellow, light
yellow, off-white (undyed), black-brown
(corroded)

symmetrical knot, V 23–24 × H 22–23 per dm
(6 × 6 per in)

EDGES: restored; main border is missing

ENDS: rewoven, stripped, new fringe added

Analysis by Walter B. Denny and
Sumru Belger Krody

39

FOUR-LEAF CLOVER USHAK-DERIVATIVE CARPET

Probably western Anatolia, late 18th or
19th century

Marshall and Marilyn R. Wolf Collection

203 × 118 cm (80 × 46 1/2 in)

In remarkably good condition, with its highly
saturated hues, including a rather strong
yellow, this carpet clearly shows its design
origins in the classical Ushak repertoire.
However, the exuberance and the peculiar
syntax of the motifs are evidence of the
creativity of Anatolian village weavers, who
rarely accepted a prototype passively but
always sought to improve it on their own terms.

WARP: wool: off-white (undyed), 2 Z-spun yarns
plied S; alternate warps slightly depressed

WEFT: wool: red, 1 Z-spun yarn; mostly 2 shoots;
discontinuous wefts cause pattern of diagonals
(lazy lines) on back of rug

PILE: wool: red, yellow, dark green, light blue-green,
dark blue, light blue, light pink-orange, off-white
(undyed), black-brown, 2 Z-spun yarns plied S

symmetrical knot, V 37 × H 31–32 per dm
(9 1/2 × 8 per in)

EDGES: re-wrapped, restored

ENDS: stripped

Analysis by Walter B. Denny and
Sumru Belger Krody

40
FOUR-LEAF CLOVER USHAK-DERIVATIVE CARPET

Central or western Anatolia, 19th century
Collection of Jon M. and Deborah Anderson
252 × 183 cm (99 × 72 in)

If the preceding carpet (cat. no. 39) shows its Ushak ancestry in both design and colors, the weaver of this example moved in a different direction. Forms are drastically simplified, the color palette is quite different, and the pile, formerly even longer and shaggier than at present, gives an entirely different visual impression.

Published: Columbus Museum of Art 1980, pl. 11

WARP: wool: off-white (undyed), 2 Z-spun yarns plied S; one level

WEFT: wool: red, 1 Z-spun yarn; 2, 3 (sometimes alternating, sometimes 2// + 1) and 4 shoots; sometimes wedges of weft, as many as eight weft-yarns wide, are woven on the edges of the rug as "shims" to even out the weave

PILE: wool: light green, dark green, red, light yellow, off-white (undyed), black-brown (slightly corroded), 2 Z-spun yarns plied S; last black-brown knot on right is tied over three warp yarns, the outermost two warp yarns being used as a pair

symmetrical knot, V 33–34 × H 25 per dm (8$^1/_2$ × 6$^1/_2$ per in)

EDGES: left: flat selvedge, weft yarn over 4 bundles of 2 warp yarns; right: flat selvedge, red weft over 5 bundles of 2 warp yarns

ENDS: bottom: 1–7 cm of red tapestry weave, stripped; top: 8 cm of red tapestry weave, flat warp braid approximately 1.5 cm wide on the left side of the carpet

Analysis by Walter B. Denny and Sumru Belger Krody

41
CARPET FRAGMENT

Probably western Anatolia, 17th century
Anonymous Collector, Pennsylvania
216 × 135 cm (85 × 53 in)

This fragment, from a so-called "bird" carpet,
represents a well-known category of white-
ground carpets, inspired by panels of white-
ground Iznik tiles and probably woven in the
Ushak area of western Anatolia. There are
other white-ground designs as well, including
the *chintamani* design exemplified in The
Textile Museum's white-ground carpet
acquired from Dumbarton Oaks (The Textile
Museum 1976.10.1; Mackie 1976, cat. no. 34).
The classical examples, such as the carpet
from which this fragment remains, were
usually woven in large sizes and often display
the border of this example, with its cloud-
bands and rosettes on vines. As with the
other Ushak classical carpets, there are many
later variants in smaller sizes, woven in
various parts of Anatolia. Not surprisingly,
the Ushak white-ground carpets were almost
always woven with a white undyed weft,
so that eventually worn patches would be
less obtrusive.

WARP: wool: off-white (undyed), 2 Z-spun yarns
plied S; one level

WEFT: wool: off-white or very light brown (undyed),
1 Z-spun yarn; 2, 3, or 4 shoots; loosely packed,
warp visible on back

PILE: wool: blue, dark green, light red, dark red,
light yellowish brown (probably once yellow),
off-white (undyed) and black-brown (corroded),
2 Z-spun yarns plied S

symmetrical knot, V 31–34 × H 28–29 per dm
(8–9 × 7–7 1/2 per in)

EDGES: restored, rewoven
ENDS: restored, rewoven

Analysis by Walter B. Denny and
Sumru Belger Krody

42
"KARA MEMI" CARPET FRAGMENT

Central Anatolia, Karapınar in Konya province, probably 18th century

Marshall and Marilyn R. Wolf Collection

120 × 99 cm (47 × 39 in)

The stylized garden flowers, popularized by the court artist Kara Memi and his followers after the middle of the 16th century, eventually found their way into the design repertoire of many different Anatolian carpets. One particular group of long, narrow carpets, utilizing the format and the characteristic colors of Karapınar in Konya province, is remarkable for its almost exclusive use of very heavily stylized flowers in its designs, evidently from a time as early as the 17th century.

Moreover, the group appears to have incorporated the motifs directly from ceramics, silk woven textiles, or embroidered textiles, as there is no evidence of earlier "classical" carpets in this design and format that might have inspired the Karapınar weavings. The archaic-seeming geometric floral forms of these carpets have sometimes lead to optimistically early dates, but a late 17th- or 18th-century date seems entirely more reasonable for most of them. Three particularly handsome early examples in the Rijksmuseum in Amsterdam (nos. 11881, 1962.11, and 1971.112) help to define the group. This fragment, in which heavily stylized tulips, carnations, hyacinths, and rosebuds can be clearly seen, is more likely to date to the late 18th century.

WARP: wool: white (undyed), 2 Z-spun yarns plied S; alternate warps slightly depressed

WEFT: wool: red, 1 Z-spun yarn; 2 or 3 (2// + 1) shoots

PILE: wool: light red, dark red, blue varying in shade (abrash), dark purple, off-white (undyed), black-brown (corroded), 2 Z-spun yarns plied S

symmetrical knot, V 28 × H 24 per dm (7 × 6 per in)

EDGES: cut

ENDS: cut

Analysis by Walter B. Denny and Sumru Belger Krody

43
"*NAZARLIK*" RUG FRAGMENT

Central or east-central Anatolia, 19th century
Marshall and Marilyn R. Wolf Collection
221 × 90 cm (87 × 35 in)

The border of this rug, probably copied
directly from an early 19th-century Ladik
rug woven in Konya province, shows
a design of tulips flanked by two leaves,
alternating with rosettes; it is a lineal
descendant of the border on the famous
16th-century Ottoman prayer rug from
The Metropolitan Museum of Art
(cat. no. 44). The four-pointed medallions
are extremely stylized descendants of
the quatrefoil medallions seen in several
examples in this exhibition (cat. nos. 20–23).

One motif of the design, found in a
significant number of central Anatolian
carpets, belongs to a different group. The
hexagons—with pendant elements hanging
both "up" and "down" and ending in a tiny
crescent—are stylized depictions of Anatolian
silver jewelry or hanging pendant balls of
glass or ceramic in mosques, which serve
to keep away the envy of malign spirits—
the "evil eye." The small pile ornaments on
the tapestry-woven skirts of some western
Anatolian carpets serve the same function.
Depictions of jewelry with hanging ornaments
are found in nomadic and village weavings
throughout the Islamic world, including
Morocco as well as the central Islamic lands
(Walker 1982, no. 8). They reflect a pervasive
element of traditional culture found not only
in the Islamic world but in non-Islamic
countries as well.

WARP: wool: off-white (undyed), 2 Z-spun yarns
plied S; one level

WEFT: wool: red, 1 Z-spun yarn; 3 shoots; loosely
packed, with warp visible on back

PILE: wool: dark brown (uncorroded), red, purple,
yellow, light blue, orange, off-white (undyed),
2 Z-spun yarns plied S

WOOL: light green, 3 Z-spun yarns plied S

symmetrical knot, V 24 × H 31–32 per cm
(6 × 8 per in)

EDGES: cut

ENDS: cut

Analysis by Walter B. Denny and
Sumru Belger Krody

44
COUPLED-COLUMN PRAYER RUG

Probably Istanbul, second half of 16th century
The Metropolitan Museum of Art, 22.100.51
The James F. Ballard Collection
Gift of James F. Ballard, 1922
168 × 127 cm (66 × 50 in)

This Ottoman prayer rug is arguably the best-known *sajjadah* in the world. Its silk foundation and Z-spun wool pile form the basis of its attribution to Istanbul or Bursa, rather than to Cairo, where so many carpets with Ottoman court designs were made, and where products are characterized by S-spun materials. Of the four basic design types of Ottoman prayer rugs, it is the only complete example of the coupled-column type to survive from the 16th century, and because of its good condition it displays all of its design elements clearly.

The border consists of eight-petalled rosettes alternating with complex floral palmettes; both are flanked by a pair of feathery leaves. The rosettes are also flanked by a pair of white tulips, while the palmettes are similarly flanked by a pair of red fan-like carnations. Each is also garnished by two sprays of hyacinths. The carefully planned borders turn the corners perfectly, with a white tulip flanked by two leaves in each corner.

The field consists of three compartments, each defined by two very thin columns, six in all, including two pairs of what have come to be called "coupled columns." The column bases are divided into facets with small, round ornaments in each, and there is a suggestion of perspective in the way they are drawn. Sprays of garden flowers, including rosebuds, carnations, and honeysuckles, occupy the three spaces between the column bases. Under the larger central arch is a depiction of a hanging lamp, in Islam a symbol of Divine Light.

The capitals are Corinthian, decorated with leaves. The spandrels of the arches are ornamented with an arabesque of *rumi* split-leaves. Above the arches is a "parapet", defined by nine ornamental merlons and two half-merlons at the side. The middle four crenelles are filled with depictions of domes on octagonal drums, again shown in an attempt at linear perspective. The other crenelles are occupied by flowers on long stems.

The secondary borders, which are also articulated at the corners, are decorated by rosettes. The guard stripes show a decoration of S-like forms linked together, an ornament common in many village and nomadic carpets, and which is found on some of the oldest surviving Anatolian carpets.

Most of these motifs, synthesized by an Ottoman court carpet designer in the late 16th century, can be seen (albeit in evolved form) among the many surviving Anatolian rugs that were influenced by this design from the 16th century through the 20th century.

Published: Dimand and Mailey, 1973, no. 105, p. 233; Ellis 1970, p. 6

WARP: silk: yellow-green, 2 slightly Z-twisted yarns plied S, and 2 slightly S-twisted yarns plied Z alternating in pairs; alternate warps slightly depressed

WEFT: silk: orange-red, spin indeterminate; 2 shoots

PILE: wool: red, dark green, yellow-green, medium yellowish-brown, dark yellowish brown, 2 Z-spun yarns probably plied S

COTTON: white (undyed), light blue, 2 Z-spun yarns probably plied S

asymmetrical knot open left, V 72 × H 60 per dm (18 × 15 per in)

EDGES: left: cut, stabilized; right: cut, restored

ENDS: stripped

Analysis by Nobuko Kajitani

45
COUPLED-COLUMN OTTOMAN
PAROKHET (TORAH CURTAIN)

Egypt, Cairo, early 17th century
The Textile Museum R16.4.4
Acquired by George Hewitt Myers in 1915
186 × 165 cm (73 × 65 in)

The Textile Museum's *parokhet* or Torah
curtain, woven in a court-controlled atelier in
Cairo to be used as a curtain in the ark of a
synagogue, shows many of the same stylistic
characteristics as The Metropolitan Museum
of Art *sajjadah* (cat. no. 44). The border
displays various types of lotus palmettes
and familiar curved leaves, but no garden
flowers. Here a single-arched field, flanked by
decorated coupled columns, utilizes the
same faceted bases and Corinthian-type
capitals. In the field, garden flowers are seen
between the column bases, and a huge
chalice symbolizing a menorah in the center
is ornamented with the traditional nine
lamps. Under the arch is a small floral spray.
In a panel above the arch is an inscription in
Hebrew from Psalms CXVIII:20—"This is
the Gate of the Lord: Through it the
Righteous Enter."

   The artistic forms shared between the
Muslim *sajjadah* and the Jewish *parokhet* are
no coincidence, for they indicate a vocabulary
of symbolism: the shared meaning of door-
like forms given to the Muslim *mihrab* and
the Jewish Torah ark, indicating a gateway to
heaven, and lamps and light as a metaphor
for God.

Published: Kühnel and Bellinger 1957, p. 53;
Ellis 1970, pp. 14–15

WARP: wool: light green, 4 S-spun yarns plied Z;
alternate warps depressed

WEFT: wool: dark red, 3 S-spun yarns plied Z;
3 shoots

PILE: wool: dark red, off-white (undyed) wool,
3 S-spun yarns plied Z

WOOL: dark green, light blue, light orange,
medium blue varying in shade (abrash), light
yellow-green wool, 2 S-spun yarns plied Z

WOOL: light yellow, medium brown (corroded),
2 Z-spun yarns plied S

asymmetrical knot open left, V 32–40 × H 31 per
dm (8–10 × 7^1/$_2$ per in)

EDGES: restored red-wool wrapping over 2 bundles
of warp yarns, each 4 S-spun yarns plied Z

ENDS: bottom: approximately 1 cm red tapestry
weave; top: cut

Analysis by Charles Grant Ellis

48
COUPLED-COLUMN *PAROKHET* (TORAH CURTAIN)

Western Anatolia, Gördes, 19th century
The Jewish Museum, New York, F5182A
Gift of Dr. Harry G. Friedman
161 × 119 cm (63¹/₂ × 47 in)

The most lavishly inscribed of all the surviving *parokhet*, this example has several Hebrew texts in addition to the large inscription from Psalms CXVIII:20 at the top of the field, which have been translated by Vivian Mann (Mann 1982, pp. 159–160). The inscriptions below the hands are from Psalms XVI:8, and those around the inner border are taken from Jeremiah XXXIII:25, Isaiah LVI:1, and I Kings VI:11, 13. The lamp contains the Tetragrammaton, the four consonants of God's name, and the praying hands bear the inscription "Almighty." At the bottom and bottom-left of the outer guard border is a dedication:

> A dedication of Judah of Avila to the holy congregation Seville, an offering of remembrance to the soul of my daughter Gracia of Avila in the year (chronogram) "And the Lord has blessed me on her account." (The numerical values of the chronogram give the Jewish year 5368, equivalent to CE 1607–1608.)

The Seville synagogue was one of the most important centers of worship of the Istanbul Sephardim. However, the date creates problems, for the carpet in question is surely a product of Gördes in western Anatolia of the 19th century, suggesting that it may have been woven to replace a much-revered earlier carpet, perhaps after the original had suffered damage of some sort, in order to perpetuate Judah d'Avila's remembrance of his daughter.

The design resemblances to the prototypes (cat. nos. 44 and 45) are quite obvious, but the bases of the columns now float weightlessly in the field. The fine Gördes weave has allowed an attempt to duplicate some aspects of the original border, and the *rumi* arabesques of the arch spandrels, while now incoherent, at least preserve the small scale and delicacy of the original.

Published: Juhansz 1989, p. 17; Mann 1982, pp. 159–160

WARP: wool: off-white (undyed), 2 Z-spun yarns plied S; alternate warps slightly depressed

WEFT: wool: red, 2 Z-spun yarns plied S; 2 shoots; cotton: white, 2 Z-spun yarns plied S; 2 shoots; discontinuous wefts cause pattern of diagonals (lazy lines) on back of rug

PILE: wool: dark blue, light blue, red, yellow, light yellowish brown, undyed off-white, black-brown (corroded), 2 Z-spun yarns plied S; cotton: white, 2 Z-spun yarns plied S

symmetrical knot, 41–43 × 41–43 per dm (10–11 × 10–11 per in)

EDGES: restored

ENDS: bottom: ³/₄ cm white taestry weave; top: 1 cm white tapestry weave

NOTE: bottom (beginning of weaving) of carpet is at top of illustration

Analysis by Walter B. Denny

49
COUPLED-COLUMN PRAYER RUG

Western Anatolia, probably Ushak, 19th century
The Textile Museum R34.22.2
Acquired by George Hewitt Myers in 1916
150.5 × 112 cm (59 × 44 in)

In this coarsely woven but colorful rug, the design of the prototype (cat. no. 44) has evolved to a simpler and more color-dominated design. The parapet, while simplified, now displays two large tulip blossoms, and the spandrels show a further geometric mutation of the *rumi* split-leaf motif. The columns are now an almost insignificant part of the design.

WARP: wool: off-white (undyed), 2 Z-spun yarns plied S; alternate warps slightly depressed

WEFT: wool: red, 1 Z-spun yarn; 2–3 shoots; discontinuous wefts cause pattern of diagonals (lazy lines) on back of rug

PILE: wool: red, light red-orange, yellow, green, blue, off-white (undyed), medium brown, black-brown

symmetrical knot, V 26–28 × H 20 per dm
(6 1/2 –7 × 5 per in)

EDGES: restored

ENDS: restored

NOTE: bottom (beginning of weaving) of carpet is at top of illustration

Analysis by Walter B. Denny and Sumru Belger Krody

50
COUPLED-COLUMN *SAFF* CARPET FRAGMENT

Western Anatolia, probably Ushak, 18th century
Marshall and Marilyn R. Wolf Collection
132 × 185.5 cm (52 × 73 in)

A number of fragments from this carpet or similar *saff* carpets, reputed to have come from the Ulu Cami (Great Mosque) of Bursa, are in other collections, including one—a gift of Don and Inge Cadle—in The Textile Museum (1996.24.1). The concept of the design, with a complex arabesque of lotus blossoms and tulips in the arch spandrels, triply cusped arches, and alternating large blue and small red field areas, is very interesting. By contrast, *saff* carpets were produced on special order in large quantities, using gifts and mosque endowment funds. The actual carpets are almost always quite coarse and are often not of the same level as the underlying design.

Published: Alexander 1993, pp. 308–09 (from same or similar example)

WARP: wool: white (undyed), 2 Z-spun yarns plied S; alternate warps slightly depressed

WEFT: wool: red, 1 Z-spun yarn; 2 shoots; discontinuous wefts cause pattern of diagonals (lazy lines) on back of rug

PILE: wool: dark blue, medium blue, green varying in shade to light blue (*abrash*), yellow, red, off-white (undyed), black-brown (corroded), 2 Z-spun yarns plied S

symmetrical knot, V 25–28 × H 20–24 per dm (6–7 × 5–6 per in)

EDGES: cut

ENDS: cut

NOTE: bottom of carpet is to left as illustrated

Analysis by Walter B. Denny and Sumru Belger Krody

51
DOUBLE-ENDED TRIPLE-ARCH DERIVATIVE CARPET

Northwestern Anatolia, 19th century
Anonymous Collector, Pennsylvania
118 × 103 cm (46½ × 40½ in)

This small carpet from northwestern Anatolia shows the ultimate evolution of the triple-arched and coupled-column *sajjadah*, as the weaver made the decision to impose both vertical and horizontal symmetry on the design. Two parapets, facing up and down, occupy the end of the field, and two sets of triple arches abut each other, while the columns have entirely disappeared. Hardly a trace of the original detailing remains; a simple and colorful northwestern Anatolian border surrounds the whole. The artistic result is as beautiful a village rug as one could imagine; a work of art that combines striking originality of design and color with a design tradition, which can be traced back almost four centuries.

WARP: wool: off-white (undyed), 2 Z-spun yarns plied S; one level

WEFT: wool: red, 1 Z-spun yarn; 2, 3 (2// + 1), 4 (2// + 2// and 3// + 1) shoots

PILE: wool: green varying in shade (*abrash*), yellow, blue, purple, red, orange, off-white (undyed), black-brown (corroded), 2 Z-spun yarns plied S

symmetrical knot, V 38–39 × H 26–27 per dm (9–10 × 6–7 per in)

EDGES: flat selvedge of 5 warp yarns wrapped in bi-colored yarn in triangular pattern

ENDS: bottom: 5 cm red tapestry weave, stripped; top: 5 cm green-and-red striped tapestry weave, 3 *nazarlık* ornaments in white-slit tapestry weave

Analysis by Walter B. Denny and Sumru Belger Krody

52
DOUBLE-ENDED TRIPLE-ARCH DERIVATIVE CARPET FRAGMENT

Probably western Anatolia, 19th century
From a Massachusetts Collector
107 × 76 cm (42 × 30 in)

In what one might describe as a full circle in evolution, the design of a double-ended triple-arch design rug (cat. no. 51) has been recombined with the notion of a single-arch *sajjadah*.

The weaver has filled the field with small ornaments in a variety of shapes, and there are numerous indications of a free and spontaneous, if not exactly precise and well-planned, approach to the weaving.

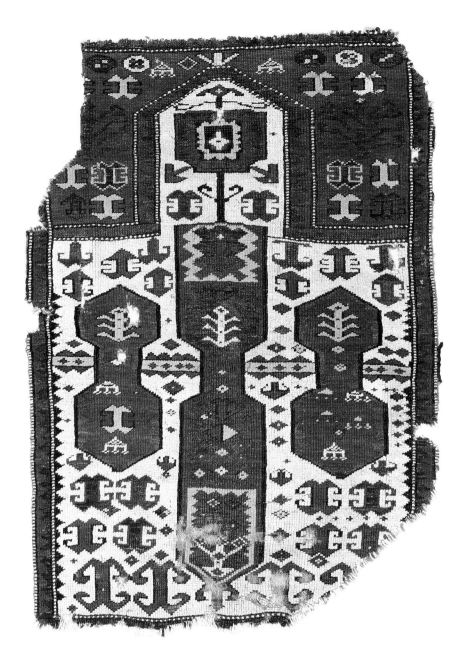

WARP: wool: white (undyed), 2 Z-spun yarns plied S; one level

WEFT: wool: red, 1 Z-spun yarn; 2–3 (2// + 1) shoots

PILE: wool: red, blue, yellow, green, off-white (undyed), black-brown (corroded), 2 Z-spun yarns plied S

symmetrical knot, V 39–41 × H 24 per dm (10–11 × 6 per in)

EDGES: fragment of selvedge on right side shows 2 warp yarns wrapped in brown-black pile wool

ENDS: cut

Analysis by Walter B. Denny

Detail of four-leaf clover Ushak-derivative
carpet, probably western Anatolia, late
18th or 19th century (cat. no. 39)

Notes

1. Denny 1979a, p. 120: "In a few decades, the handweaving of rugs as a viable commercial enterprise and as an integral part of traditional society will be a memory."

2. For a general appraisal of the importance of the Anatolian tradition see King and Sylvester 1983 and Erdmann 1977. The collection of papers in Pinner and Denny 1986, the result of a symposium organized, commissioned, assembled, and coordinated by Robert Pinner, remain the most important single work on the subject published in the last 40 years.

3. Erdmann 1970, pp. 41–46.

4. Balpınar and Hirsch 1988, pp. 34–40 and 178–181; the substance of these arguments was first articulated in 1984 (Balpınar ms.). Although the visual comparisons used by Balpınar may be flawed, in the ensuing 18 years since her first presentation on the subject I have become convinced that her dating of these two carpets is fundamentally correct, and that they are the two oldest Anatolian carpets known.

5. Arseven 1952, pp. 15–40; Barthels 1985. A major blow to the "place" partisans occurred when the claims of James Mellaart to have discovered extremely ancient wall paintings, showing what appeared to be Anatolian kilim designs at Çatal Höyük, proved to be fraudulent.

6. Amirian 1981, p. 31; Sassouni 1981.

7. Denny 1982; Böhmer and Brüggerman 1983, among others.

8. Saunders 1981, especially the articles by Murray Eiland and Michael David.

9. Many of the original appellations were coined by Wilhelm von Bode in the late 19th century (Bode and Kühnel 1922) and have been confirmed in subsequent general carpet histories. The most important research on carpets in European paintings has been done in a series of articles by John Mills (Mills 1981; Mills 1986; Mills 1991).

10. Erdmann 1970, pp. 41–46; Erdmann 1977, pp. 7–26; Aslanapa and Durul 1973, where all are illustrated.

11. See note 4.

12. The British scholar Michael Ryder, author of *Sheep and Man* (London, 1983), has been a pioneer in efforts to put fiber research in the service of carpet scholarship. See, for example, Ryder 1987a, pp. 20–21 and Ryder 1987b, p. 10.

13. Böhmer and Thompson 1991, pp. 30–36.

14. Moshkova 1980, pp. 16–26; Mackie and Thompson 1980, pp. 64–82.

15. Beattie 1978, p. 30; Pope 1981, p. 2452.

16. Balpınar and Hirsch 1988, pls. 4–5; Ölçer and Denny 1999, nos. 26–34. For an interesting extended discussion of this matter, see Böhmer and Brüggeman 1983, pp. 45–70.

17. Thompson 1980.

18. For the art-historical arguments, see Denny 1982. For the historical evidence of Türkmen movements see Sümer 1992. For a full discussion of the Türkmen tribes and their art, see Mackie and Thompson 1980.

19. An especially interesting study of the way that artisans moved from place to place is to be found in Meinecke 1976, the doctoral dissertation of the late Michael Meinecke.

20. Vakıflar Museum, Istanbul A-217, illustrated in Balpınar and Hirsch 1988, pp. 28–41, cat. nos. 1–2.

21. King and Sylvester 1983; Erdmann 1962.

22. Kühnel and Bellinger 1957.

23. Briggs 1940; Briggs 1946.

24. Woods 1999.

25. Denny 1978, pp. 156–164; King and Sylvester 1983, p. 85.

26. Purportedly discovered in Tibet, the carpet was for some time in the possession of the dealer Jeremy Pine, and is now in the collection of Sheikh Saud al-Thani of Qatar.

27. Barbaro and Contarini 1873 [1478], p. 60.

28. The *Divan* of Hidayat in the Chester Beatty Library (manuscript 401, with four tiny miniatures), coincidentally dated to 1478, has no clear depictions of carpet design, although the medallion designs of its elegant outer binding and doublure would make lovely carpets (Minorsky 1958, pp. 1–3).

29. Istanbul, Topkapı Palace Museum Library, Album H. 2153, folio 91A.

30. Kühnel and Bellinger 1957, p. 77–78; Spuhler 1986, p. 266–267; Ellis 1988, pp. 4–7.

31. Museum für Angewandte Kunst, Vienna T 8348 1922 KB, illustrated in Völker 2001, no. 1.

32. MFA, Boston 65.595, illustrated in King and Sylvester 1983, p. 85.

33. Philadelphia Museum of Art 55-65-2, illustrated in Ellis 1988, p. 5.

34. Museum für Islamische Kunst, Berlin I.33/60, illustrated in Spuhler 1987, pl. 74.

35. Several fragments have been reunited in the Museum für Angewandte Kunst, Vienna; see the discussion by Dr. Angela Völker in Völker 2001, pp. 36–41.

36. Museum für Islamische Kunst, Berlin 86,601, illustrated in Spuhler 1987, p. 216.

37. Vakıflar Museum, Istanbul A-172 and A-216, illustrated in Balpınar and Hirsch 1988, pp. 293 and 295.

38. TIEM Inv. Nos. 869-844-850-846, illustrated in Ölçer, Enderlein, Batári, and Mills 1996; and 845-847-848-849-851-868, illustrated in Ölçer and Denny 1999, pl. 1.

39. Museum für Islamische Kunst, Berlin I.5526; see Spuhler 1987, cat. 4.

40. TIEM Inv. No. 468; illustrated in Ölçer, Enderlein, Batári, and Mills 1996, pl. 42 and detail.

41. For examples, see Ölçer, Enderlein, Batári, and Mills 1996, pls. 40 (TIEM Inv. No. 701), 41 (TIEM Inv. No. 694), 42 (TIEM Inv. No. 468), 43 (TIEM Inv. No. 312), and 46 (TIEM Inv. No. 329).

42. Denny 1982, ill. 18; Völker 2001, pp. 42–45.

43. TIEM Inv. Nos. 694 and 329; see Ölçer, Enderlein, Batári, and Mills 1996, pls. 41 and 46.

44. Denny, 1982, ill. 1; Mackie and Thompson 1980, cat. nos. 9 and 14.

45. Walker 1979, pp. 115–116 and back cover.

46. Mackie and Thompson 1980, p. 110, no. 38.

47. Opie 1981, p. 139; Tanavoli 1985, pp. 89–90.

48. Batári 1994, p. 96; Ölçer, Enderlein, Batári, and Mills 1996, pls. 56 and 58. See also in the same volume pls. 57 and 65 for two other somewhat later examples.

49. Erdmann 1962, pl. 16.

50. Balpınar ms.

51. The painting is reproduced in Balpınar and Hirsch 1988, p. 31, pl. 18.

52. Ölçer, Enderlein, Batári, and Mills 1996, pl. 18, and Batári 1994, pl. 1 for the carpet fragment; the soumak, probably of the 18th or early 19th century, is illustrated in Batári n.d., cat. no. 9.

53. See the full discussion of the "keyhole" motif by Ellis 1988, pp. 77–79.

54. Mills 1991, p. 89.

55. Ellis 1988, pp. 80–91, for several examples of small medallion carpets with quatrefoil medallions.

56. The eponym is painted in a famous altarpiece of 1542 known as the *Charity of Saint Anthony*, in the church of SS Giovanni e Paolo in Venice (which incidentally also includes a depiction of a very handsome "para-Mamluk" carpet), Brown, Humphrey, and Lucco 1998, p. 8 and pp. 59–68.

57. Ellis 1975; Ellis 1988, pp. 22–39.

58. Végh and Layer 1977, pls. 3–5; Batári 1994, pp. 101–113.

59. The first major contribution to this subject is Paquin's electronically published article (Paquin 1996), originally given as a conference paper in 1994. Much of the same material was then covered in print by Christina Klose in the publication of her conference presentation in Philadelphia in 1996 (Klose 1999). The same subject is dealt with on a more restricted scale by Walter B. Denny in Ölçer and Denny 1999, vol. I, pp. 50–55.

60. TIEM Inv. No. 688. The Chinese origins of the design were first pointed out by Agnes Geijer (Geijer 1963, p. 83). In the same article Geijer was also the first to suggest that the "Konya" carpets were not "original equipment" in the 13th-century mosque in which they were found (as Erdmann argued), but were in fact from the following century. TIEM Inv. No. 688 was later discussed by Louise W. Mackie in connection with a 15th-century Spanish carpet in The Textile Museum, which in turn reproduces the Turkish carpet's design (Mackie 1977, pp. 28–30). The TIEM carpet has been reproduced most recently in Ölçer, Enderlein, Batári, and Mills 1996, pl. 4.

61. The best and most recent discussion of this matter is by Louise W. Mackie in Atasoy, Denny, Mackie, and Tezcan 2001, pp. 197 ff.

62. Raby and Tanındı 1993, pp. 174–5 and 178–9; Atasoy, Denny, Mackie, and Tezcan 2001, p. 240, pls. 11–12.

63. Atasoy, Denny, Mackie, and Tezcan 2001, p. 204 and pp. 270–290.

64. Carpets in the "floral" version are far rarer, no doubt due to the complexity of the designs. A few Ushak carpets using ogival layouts copied directly from Ottoman textiles of the later 16th century were discovered in the 1960s in the mosque of Mihrimah in the Üsküdar quarter of Istanbul. One was published (erroneously, as a "multiple-niche prayer carpet") in Ölçer, Enderlein, Batári, and Mills 1996, pl. 126.

65. Raby 1986a and Raby 1986b.

66. Raby and Tanındı 1993.

67. Boralevi 1987.

68. Suriano 2001, pp. 106–115.

69. Erdmann 1976, pp. 31–33. In assessing the importance of Kurt Erdmann's many contributions to the study of carpets it is important to remember that, at the time that he was doing some of his most seminal work, he had no access to most of the great Istanbul collections, whose contents are so important for the study of carpet history (see R. Pinner in his preface to Erdmann 1977, which was originally published in 1957). Putting Erdmann's work in perspective magnifies the nature of his accomplishment.

70. Erdmann's hypothesis was further explored by Susan Day in Day 1999, which attempted to focus on the relationship between Timurid miniature paintings and Safavid carpets. Curiously and significantly, however, when Day attempted to compare actual carpets to the representations in miniature paintings, three of her closest comparisons involved not Safavid carpets but Ushak carpets.

71. Day 1999.

72. Raby 1986a; Raby 1986b.

73. Raby and Tanındı 1993, pp. 54–79.

74. Denny 1979b, p.10; Raby and Tanındı 1993, p. 23; Ölçer and Denny 1999, vol. I, p. 6.

75. Ydema 1991, pp. 41–45. Ydema employed statistical method and computer technology to measure the appearance of various carpet types in the Netherlandish paintings by decade, and the results are in many cases quite revealing about European taste and the European market for various groups of Islamic carpets from Turkey, Iran, and India.

76. Both in the Süleymaniye Library in Istanbul: Şehzade Mehmed 28 and Süleymaniye 1025 (Raby 1986, p. 184, ills. 14–15).

77. Raby 1986b, p. 185.

78. Actually named the Masjid-i Muzaffariyah, the building was erected for the Kara Koyunlu king Abu'l Muzaffar Jahanshah, who was killed and whose dynasty was then supplanted by the rival Ak Koyunlu dynasty in 1468, just three years after the structure's completion (Golombek and Wilber 1988, vol. 1, pp. 407–409).

79. Erdmann 1963, p. 95, fig. 8.

80. An interesting group of Ushak medallion carpets published together, which demonstrates the variety and diversity within the Ushak manufacturing area by its many differences in color

and design, can be found in Ölçer and Denny 1999, vol. II, pls. 52–64. The lengths of these carpets vary from about 300 cm to well over 100 cm. See also Balpınar and Hirsch 1988, pls. 43–46 for another group of medallion carpets from one collection, and Lanier 1975, pls. 28–33 for another with a much broader chronological range. It should be noted that few today would accept the doubts (originating with Charles Grant Ellis and May Beattie) about the date of Williamsburg 1953-571 (Lanier 1975, pl. 33).

81. Ölçer and Denny 1999, vol. I, Chapter 7; Balpınar and Hirsch 1988, pls. 27–38 and 47.

82. Erdmann 1963, ills. 1–4, catalogued by Erdmann as types I (all medallions the same) and II (two alternating forms of medallion).

83. Erdmann 1963, p. 90, ills. 5, where they are catalogued as Type III.

84. Ölçer and Denny 1999, vol. I, pp. 42–43.

85. For a full discussion of Ottoman court carpets, see Denny 1979b and 1986. The technical characteristics of Ottoman court carpets are discussed in Kühnel and Bellinger 1957 and Ellis 1970.

86. Denny 1973, p. 10, figs. 5–6.

87. Denny 1973, p. 12, figs. 10–11.

88. Important work on the *saz* style has been done in Turkish by Dr. Banu Mahir and Dr. Filiz Çağman. For a well-illustrated discussion of examples, see Atıl 1987, pp. 97–109.

89. Atıl 1987, pp. 55–56.

90. Other examples are mentioned in the text of catalogue number 42.

91. Ölçer and Denny 1999, p. 38.

92. Mackie 1976, pp. 5–20.

93. Walker 1982, no. 8; Böhmer and Brüggeman 1983, nos. 106–107.

94. For a discussion of both *saff* carpets and *sajjadah*s, see Denny 1989.

95. In addition to the discussion in Denny 1989, see Ettinghausen 1974 for an extended discussion of the *sajjadah* in its many manifestations, both in Anatolia and elsewhere. Symbolism of the prayer rug is also discussed by the various authors in Blair and Bloom 1991. Finally, a large number of Anatolian *sajjadah*, including many never previously published, are illustrated in Ölçer and Denny 1999.

96. Ettinghausen, Dimand, Mackie, and Ellis 1974; Denny 1989.

97. The Ottoman court prayer rugs are discussed in detail in

Ellis 1969; examples that have come to light more recently are discussed by Denny and Walker 1988, and are mentioned in Atıl 1990, no. 106.

98. Indications for placement of feet may be seen in Ölçer, Enderlein, Batári, and Mills 1996, no. 125, and in Ölçer and Denny 1999, no. 103. Depictions of hands, more common in Transcaucasian *sajjadah*, can be seen in Ettinghausen 1977, no. XXXIII. Their use in torah curtains is common; see Juhasz 1989, pp. 113–115.

99. Ölçer and Denny 1999, vol. I, pl. 2, and vol. II, pp. 57–58.

100. Böhmer and Brüggeman 1983, pp. 79–81.

101. Most common in rugs from western Anatolia, the phenomenon is seen however in many different weaving traditions. See Denny and Walker 1988, pls. 19 and 21.

102. An excellent example showing "picked" flowers at the top is illustrated in McMullan, *et al.* 1970, no. 19.

103. Dimand and Mailey 1973, cat. no. 105; also discussed in Ellis 1969, Denny 1986 and Denny 1989.

104. Beattie 1979 for perhaps the best-known discussion of the evolution of the form. Examples can be seen in Batári 1994, pls. 66–77 and Ölçer and Denny 1999, pls. 94–98.

105. Denny 1986 for a discussion of the emergence of the Kara Memi style.

106. For discussions of the 1585 documents, see Denny 1986, and Erdmann 1938, p. 179 ff.

107. Blair and Bloom 1991, nos. 22A–23b; also Denny 1989, p. 102, which poses the question dealt with here without answering it; a well-known representation of the triple gateway to Paradise executed in Herat around 1430 is illustrated in Séguy 1977, pl. 39.

108. Mann, Glick, and Dodds 1992, p. 247, for a full discussion of this matter, in connection with a famous Spanish pile carpet probably woven as a pew cover for a synagogue.

109. *Ibid.*

110. Ölçer and Denny 1999, pl. 2.

111. Atıl 1990, pp. 296–297 and Denny and Walker 1988, p. 57, for two well-known examples.

112. Felton 1997, no. 93.

113. Boralevi 1984; Boralevi 1986.

114. For the most comprehensive discussion of the motif, see Paquin 1992, pp. 104 ff.

115. Felton 1997, pp. 160–177; Juhasz 1989, pp. 100–101 and pls. 18–19; Mann 1982, nos. 197–198.

Bibliography

Alexander, Christopher, 1993, *A Foreshadowing of 21st Century Art: The Color and Geometry of Very Early Turkish Carpets*. Oxford University Press, New York, and Oxford.

Amirian, Lemyel, 1981, On the Dragon and Phoenix Rug in Berlin, *Hali*, vol. IV, no. 1, p. 31. Hali Publications Ltd., London.

Arseven, Celâl Esad, 1952, *Les arts decoratifs turcs*. Millî Eğitim Basımevi, İstanbul.

Aslanapa, Oktay, and Yusuf Durul, 1973, *Selçuklu Halıları*. Ak Yayınları, İstanbul.

Atasoy, Nurhan, Walter B. Denny, Louise W. Mackie, and Hülya Tezcan, 2001, *İpek: Imperial Ottoman Silks and Velvets*. Azimuth Editions, London.

Atıl, Esin, 1987, *The Age of Sultan Suleyman the Magnificent*. National Gallery of Art, Washington, and H. Abrams, New York.

Atıl, Esin (editor), 1990, *Islamic Art and Patronage: Treasures from Kuwait*. Rizzoli, New York.

Balpınar, Belkis, ms., The Oldest Turkish Carpets. Paper presented at the First International Congress of Turkish Carpets, Istanbul, October 9, 1984.

Balpınar, Belkis, and Udo Hirsch, 1988, *Carpets of the Vakıflar Museum, İstanbul*. Uta Hülsey, Wesel.

Barbaro, Josafa, and Ambrogio Contarini, 1873, *Travels to Tana and Persia*. Translated from the Italian by William Thomas. Originally published in 1478, London.

Barthels, Herwig, 1985, On the Origins of Anatolian Kilim Designs, *Oriental Carpet and Textile Studies I*, pp. 202–210. Edited by Robert Pinner and Walter B. Denny. Hali Magazine, London.

Batári, Ferenc, n.d., *Caucasian Rugs: Exhibition in the Gallery in Miskolc from the Collection of the Museum of Applied Art, Budapest*. Museum of Applied Art, Budapest.

1994, *Ottoman Turkish Carpets*. Keszthely, Budapest.

Beattie, May H., 1972, *The Thyssen-Bornemisza Collection of Oriental Rugs*. Villa Favorita and Thyssen-Bornemisza Collection, Castagnola and Ticino.

1979, Some Motifs in Anatolian Rugs—Ancestors and Descendants, *Hali*, vol. II, no. 2, Summer, pp. 101–105. Hali Publications, London.

Beattie, May H. (editor), 1978, *Carpets of Central Persia with Special Reference to Rugs of Kirman: Proceedings of the Colloquium*. Sheffield City Art Galleries, Sheffield.

Biedroñska-Słotowa, Beata, 1986, *Kobierce Tureckie (Turkish Carpets)*. Printed by National Printing Press, The National Museum, Kraków.

Bier, Carol, 1996a, Legacy of Collector George Hewitt Myers, *Arts of Asia*, vol. 26, no. 1, January/February, pp. 58–65. Arts of Asia Publications Ltd., Hong Kong.

1996b, Approaches to Understanding Oriental Carpets, *Arts of Asia*, vol. 26, no. 1, January/February, pp. 66–81. Arts of Asia Publications Ltd., Hong Kong.

Blair, Sheila S., and Jonathan M. Bloom (editors), 1991, *Images of Paradise in Islamic Art*. Hood Museum of Art, Dartmouth College, Hanover.

Bode, Wilhelm von, and Ernst Kühnel, 1922, *Antique Rugs from the Near East*. Third Revised Edition, translated by Rudolph M. Riefstahl. E. Weyhe, New York.

Böhmer, Harald, and Werner Brüggeman, 1983, *Rugs of the Peasants and Nomads of Anatolia*. Kunst and Antiquitaten, Munich.

Böhmer, Harald, and Jon Thompson, 1991, The Pazyryk Carpet: A Technical Discussion, *Source: Notes in the History of Art*, vol. X, no. 4 , Summer, pp. 30–36. Ars Brevis, New York.

Boralevi, Alberto, 1984, Un tappeto Ebraico Italo-Egiziano, *Critica d'Arte*, vol. XLIX, no. 2, July–September, pp. 34–47. Sansoni, Florence.

1986, Three Egyptian Carpets in Italy, *Oriental Carpet and Textile Studies II: Carpets of the Mediterranean Countries 1400–1600*, pp. 205–220. Edited by Robert Pinner and Walter B. Denny. Hali OCTS Ltd., London.

1987, *l'Ushak Castellani-Stroganoff ed Altri Tappeti Ottomani dal XVI al XVIII Secolo*. KARTA snc, Florence.

Brancati, Luca, ms., Genoa and Carpets: Documents and Figurative Evidence from Animal Carpets to "Holbein Large Pattern" Ones. Paper presented at the Second International Congress on Turkish and Central Asian Carpets, Istanbul, October 15, 1994.

Briggs, Amy, 1940, Timurid Carpets, *Ars Islamica*, vol. VII, pp. 20–54. The Research Seminary in Islamic Art, Institute of Fine Arts, University of Michigan, Ann Arbor.

1946, Timurid Carpets, *Ars Islamica*, vols. XI–XII, pp. 146–158. The Research Seminary in Islamic Art, Institute of Fine Arts, University of Michigan, Ann Arbor.

Brown, David Alan, Peter Humphrey, and Mauro Lucco (editors), 1998, *Lorenzo Lotto: Rediscovered Master of the Renaissance*. National Gallery of Art, Washington, New Haven, and London.

Cahen, Claude, 1968, *Pre-Ottoman Turkey: A General Survey of the Material of a Spiritual Culture and History, c. 1071–1330*. Translated from the French by J. Jones-Williams. Taplinger, New York.

Columbus Museum of Art, 1980, *Looms of Splendor: Oriental Rugs from Columbus Collections*. Columbus Museum of Art, Columbus.

Christie's London, 1996, *Important Classical and Turkish Rugs and Carpets*. Sale LIAISON-5699, Thursday, 17 October. Christie's, London.

2000, *Oriental Rugs and Carpets*. Sale LOOT-6283, Thursday, 13 April. Christie's, London.

2001, *Davide Halevin: Magnificent Carpets and Tapestries*. Sale HALEVIM-6423, Wednesday, 14 February. Christie's, London.

Collins, Sheridan Pressey, 1985, George Hewitt Myers, *Hali*, issue 27, vol. 7, no. 3, July/August/September, pp. 6–7. Hali Publications Ltd., London.

Day, Susan, ms., *Catalogue raisonné des tapis mamlouks et ottomans du Musée des Arts Dècoratifs Paris*. M.A. thesis, École du Louvre, Paris, 1985.

1999, Paradise Gained: Timurid Painting as the Mainspring of Safavid Carpet Design, *Oriental Carpet and Textile Studies V*, Part 1, pp. 7–17. Edited by Murray L. Eiland, Jr. and Robert Pinner. International Conference on Oriental Carpets, Danville.

Denny, Walter B., 1973, Anatolian Rugs: An Essay on Method, *The Textile Museum Journal*, vol. 3, no 4, December, pp. 7–25. The Textile Museum, Washington.

1978, Ten Great Carpets in the Museum of Fine Arts, Boston, *Hali*, vol. I, no. 2, pp. 156–164. Hali Publications Ltd., London.

1979a, *Oriental Rugs*. Cooper-Hewitt Museum, The Smithsonian Institution, New York.

1979b, Origin of the Designs of Ottoman Court Carpets. *Hali*, vol. II, issue. 1, Spring, pp. 6–11. Hali Publications Ltd., London.

1982, Turkoman Rugs and the Origins of Rug Weaving in the Western Islamic World, *Hali*, vol. 4, no. 4, pp. 329–337. Hali Publications Ltd., London.

ms., Turkish Carpets and Ottoman Architecture. Paper presented at the First International Conference on Turkish Carpets, Istanbul, October 8, 1984.

1986, The Origin and Development of Ottoman Court Carpets, *Oriental Carpet and Textile Studies II: Carpets of the Mediterranean Countries 1400–1600*, p. 243–260. Edited by Robert Pinner and Walter B. Denny. Hali OCTS Ltd., London.

1987, Connoisseur's Choice: The G. H. Myers Coupled-Column Prayer Rug, *Hali*, issue 33, vol. 9, no.1, January/February/March, pp. 8–9. Hali Publications Ltd., London.

1989, *Saff* and *Sajjadah*: Origins and Meaning of the Prayer Rug, *Oriental Carpet and Textile Studies III*, pp. 93–104. Edited by Robert Pinner and Walter B. Denny. Islamic Department of Sotheby's and Hali OCTS Ltd., London.

ms., The Turkish Large-Octagon Carpets of the 15th and 16th Centuries: Origins, Development and Meaning of the Large-Pattern Holbeins. Paper presented at the Sixth International Conference on Oriental Carpets, San Francisco, November 18, 1990.

ms., The Turkoman Style and the Carpet Design Revolution. Paper presented at the Second International Congress on Turkish and Central Asian Carpets, Istanbul, October 15, 1994.

Denny, Walter B., and Daniel Walker, 1988, *The Markarian Album: The Richard R. Markarian Collection of Oriental Rugs*. The Markarian Foundation, Cincinnati.

Dimand, Maurice S., 1935, *The Ballard Collection of Oriental Rugs in the City Art Museum of St. Louis*. Berenice C. Ballard and Nellie Ballard White, St. Louis.

Dimand, Maurice S., and Jean Mailey, 1973, *Oriental Rugs in The Metropolitan Museum of Art*. The Metropolitan Museum of Art, New York.

Ellis, Charles Grant, 1970, The Ottoman Prayer Rugs. *The Textile Museum Journal*, vol. 2, no. 4, December 1969, pp. 5–22. The Textile Museum, Washington.

1975, The 'Lotto' Pattern as a Fashion in Carpets. *Festschrift für Wilhelm Meister*, pp. 19–31. Dr. Ernst Hauswedell & Co., Hamburg.

1986, On 'Holbein' and 'Lotto' Rugs, *Oriental Carpet and Textile Studies II: Carpets of the Mediterranean Countries 1400–1600*, pp. 163–176. Edited by Robert Pinner and Walter B. Denny. Hali OCTS Ltd., London.

1988, *Oriental Carpets in the Philadelphia Museum of Art*. Philadelphia Museum of Art, Philadelphia.

Erdmann, Kurt, 1938, Kairener Teppiche, Teil I: Europäische und Islamische Quellen des 15–18 Jahrhunderts, *Ars Islamica*, vol. 5, pp. 179–206. The Research Seminary in Islamic Art, Institute of Fine Arts, University of Michigan, Ann Arbor.

1959, Ka'bah Fliesen, *Ars Orientalis*, vol. III, pp. 192–197. Freer Gallery of Art, Smithsonian Institution, Washington, and Fine Arts Department, University of Michigan, Ann Arbor.

1962, *Europa und der Orientteppich*. F. Kupfernerg, Berlin and Mainz.

1963, Weniger bekannte Uschak-Muster, *Kunst des Orients*, vol. IV, pp. 79–97. F. Steiner, Wiesbaden.

1970, *Seven Hundred Years of Oriental Carpets*. Edited by H. Erdmann, translated by M. Beattie and H. Herzog. University of California Press, Berkeley and Los Angeles.

1976, *Oriental Carpets: An Account of Their History*. Translated by Charles Grant Ellis. Universe Books, New York.

1977, *The History of the Early Turkish Carpet*. Translated by Robert Pinner and Bibliography of Kurt Erdmann on carpets compiled by Hanna Erdmann. Oğuz Press, London.

Ettinghausen, Richard, Maurice S. Dimand, Louise Mackie, and Charles Grant Ellis, 1974, *Prayer Rugs*. The Textile Museum, Washington.

Farnham, Thomas J., 2001, Bardini, Classical Carpets, and America, *Hali*, issue 119, November/December, pp. 75–85. Hali Publications Ltd., London.

Felton, Anton, 1997, *Jewish Carpets: A History and Guide*. Antique Collectors' Club, Woodbridge, Suffolk.

Franses, Michael, and John Eskenasi, 1996, *Turkish Rugs and Old Master Paintings*. Author-published, London.

Geijer, Agnes, 1963, Some Thoughts on the Problems of Early Oriental Carpets, *Ars Orientalis*, vol. V, pp.79–87. Freer Gallery of Art, Smithsonian Institution, Washington, and Fine Arts Department, University of Michigan, Ann Arbor.

Golombek, Lisa, and D. Wilber, 1988, *The Timurid Architecture of Iran and Turan*. 2 vols. Princeton University Press, Princeton.

Hali, 1996a, Asian Harvest, Auction Previews, Marketplace, *Hali*, issue 88, p. 148. Hali Publications Ltd., London.

1996b, Marketplace, *Hali*, issue 89, November, p. 140. Hali Publications Ltd., London.

1997, Marketplace, Auction Price Guide, *Hali*, issue 90, January, pp. 120–121. Hali Publications Ltd., London.

2001, Auction Price Guide, *Hali*, issue 116, May/June, p. 156. Hali Publications Ltd., London.

İnalcık, Halil, 1986, The Yürüks: Their Origins, Expansion and Economic Role, *Oriental Carpet and Textile Studies II: Carpets of the Mediterranean Countries 1400–1600*, pp. 39–65. Edited by Robert Pinner and Walter B. Denny. Hali OCTS Ltd., London.

Irwin, Robert G., 1986, Egypt, Syria and their Trading Partners 1450–1550, *Oriental Carpet and Textile Studies II: Carpets of the Mediterranean Countries 1400–1600*, pp. 73–82. Edited by Robert Pinner and Walter B. Denny. Hali OCTS Ltd., London.

Juhasz, Esther (editor), 1989, *Sephardi Jews in the Ottoman Empire: Aspects of Material Culture*. The Israel Museum, Jerusalem.

King, Donald, and David Sylvester, 1983, *The Eastern Carpet in the Western World From the 15th to the 17th Century*. Arts Council of Great Britain, London.

Kirchheim, Heinrich, and Michael Franses, Friedrich Spuhler, Garry Muse, Jürg Rageth, Eberhart Hermann, 1993, *Orient Stars: A Carpet Collection*. E. Heinrich Kirchheim and Hali Publications Ltd., London.

Klose, Christina, 1999, Textiles as Models for Turkish Carpets of the 16th and 17th Centuries, *Oriental Carpet and Textile Studies V*, Part 1, pp. 47–52. Edited by Murray L. Eiland, Jr. and Robert Pinner. International Conference on Oriental Carpets, Danville.

Kühnel, Ernst, and Louisa Bellinger, 1957, *Cairene Rugs and Others Technically Related (15th–17th Century)*. The Textile Museum, Washington.

Lanier, Mildred B., 1975, *English and Oriental Carpets at Williamsburg*. The Colonial Williamsburg Foundation, Williamsburg.

Lukens, Petronel, ms., *Notes about the Textile Museum*, 40 pp. The Textile Museum, Washington, 1973.

Mack, Rosamond, 1998, Lotto: A Carpet Connoisseur, *Lorenzo Lotto: Rediscovered Master of the Renaissance*, pp. 59–68, Edited by David Alan Brown, Peter Humphrey, and Mauro Lucco. National Gallery of Art, Washington, New Haven, and London.

Mackie, Louise, 1974, *The Splendor of Turkish Weavings*. The Textile Museum, Washington.

1976, A Turkish Carpet with Spots and Stripes, *The Textile Museum Journal*, vol. IV, no. 3, pp. 5–20. The Textile Museum, Washington.

1977, Two Remarkable Fifteenth-Century Carpets from Spain, *The Textile Museum Journal*, vol. 4, no. 4, pp. 15–32. The Textile Museum, Washington.

Mackie, Louise W., and Jon Thompson (editors), 1980, *Turkmen Tribal Carpets and Traditions*. The Textile Museum, Washington.

Mann, Vivian B. (editor), 1982, *A Tale of Two Cities: Jewish Life in Frankfurt and Istanbul 1750–1870*. The Jewish Museum, New York.

Mann, Vivian B., Thomas F. Glick, and Jerrilyn D. Dodds (editors), 1992, *Convivencia: Jews, Muslims, and Christians in Medieval Spain*. George Braziller in association with The Jewish Museum, New York.

McMullan, Joseph V., 1965, *Islamic Carpets*. With a forward by Ernst J. Grube, photographs by Otto E. Nelson. Near Eastern Art Research Center, Inc., New York.

McMullan, Joseph V., et al.,s.d, *The George Walter Vincent and Belle Townsley Smith Collection of Islamic Rugs*. Springfield, 1970.

Meinecke, Michael, 1976, *Fayencedekorationen seldschukischer Sakralbauten in Kleinasien*. 2 vols. Wasmuth, Tübingen.

Mills, John, 1981, 'Lotto' Carpets in Western Paintings, *Hali*, vol. 3, |no. 4, pp. 278–89. Hali Publications Ltd., London.

1986, Near Eastern Carpets in Italian Paintings, *Oriental Carpet and Textile Studies II: Carpets of the Mediterranean Countries 1400–1600*, pp. 109–122. Edited by Robert Pinner and Walter B. Denny. Hali OCTS Ltd., London.

1991, Carpets in Paintings: the 'Bellini,' 'Keyhole' or 'Re-entrant' Rugs, *Hali*, issue. 58, vol. 13, no. 4, August, pp. 86–103. Hali Publications Ltd., London.

Minorsky, Vladimir, 1958, *The Chester Beatty Library: A Catalogue of the Turkish Manuscripts and Miniatures*. Hodges, Figgis, Dublin.

Moshkova, V. G., 1980, The Tribal Göl in Turkoman Carpets, *Turkoman Studies I*, pp. 16–26. Edited by Robert Pinner and Michael Franses. Oguz Press, London.

Myers, George Hewitt, 1931, The Washington Textile Museum, *The American Magazine of Art*, vol. XXII, no. 5, pp. 335–345. The American Federation of Arts, Washington.

Necipoğlu, Gülru, 1995, *The Topkapı Scroll—Geometry and Ornament in Islamic Architecture*. The Getty Center for the History of Art and the Humanities, Santa Monica.

Ölçer, Nazan, and Volkmar Enderlein, Ferenc Batári, John Mills, 1996, *Turkish Carpets from the 13th–18th Centuries*. Technical analyses by Nils Rüters. Ahmet Ertuğ, İstanbul.

Ölçer, Nazan, and Walter B. Denny, 1999, *Anatolian Carpets: Master-pieces from the Museum of Turkish and Islamic Art, Istanbul*. Photographs by Ahmet Ertuğ, 2 vols. Ertuğ and Kocabıyık, Bern.

Opie, James, 1981, *Tribal Rugs of Southern Persia*. Oriental Rugs Inc., Portland.

Paquin, Gerard, 1992, *Çintamani*. *Hali*, issue 64, vol. 14, no. 4, August, pp. 104–119. Hali Publications Ltd., London.

1996, *Silk and Wool: Ottoman Textile Design in Turkish Rugs*. Paper presented at the 2nd International Congress on Turkish Carpets, İstanbul, in October 1994. Published on the Internet at http://jefferson.village.Virginia.EDU/~jmu2m/gp/

Pinner, Robert, 1986, Appendix: References to Carpet Production and Trade "and" Designs of Carpets listed in Inventories, *Oriental Carpet and Textile Studies II: Carpets of the Mediterranean Countries 1400–1600*, pp. 291–306. Edited by Robert Pinner and Walter B. Denny. Hali OCTS Ltd., London.

Pinner, Robert and Walter B. Denny (editors), 1986, *Oriental Carpet and Textile Studies II: Carpets of the Mediterranean Countries 1400–1600*. Hali OCTS Ltd., London.

Pitcher, Donald Edgar, 1972, *An Historical Geography of the Ottoman Empire*. Brill, Leiden.

Pope, A. U., 1981, The Technique of Persian Carpet Weaving, *Survey of Persian Art VI*, pp. 2437–2455. Edited by A. U. Pope and P. Ackerman. Third Edition, Second Impression. Originally published by Oxford University Press, London, 1938–1939. Personally Oriented Ltd., Ashiya.

Raby, Julian, 1986a, Court and Export: Part I. Market Demands in Ottoman Carpets 1450–1550, *Oriental Carpet and Textile Studies II: Carpets of the Mediterranean Countries 1400–1600*, pp. 29–38. Edited by Robert Pinner and Walter B. Denny. Hali OCTS Ltd., London.

1986b, Court and Export: Part 2. The Uşak Carpets, *Oriental Carpet and Textile Studies II: Carpets of the Mediterranean Countries 1400–1600*, pp. 177–187. Edited by Robert Pinner and Walter B. Denny. Hali OCTS Ltd., London.

Raby, Julian, and Zeren Tanındı, 1993, *Bookbinding in the 15th Century: The Foundation of an Ottoman Court Style*, Azimuth Editions, London.

Rogers, Michael, 1986, Carpets in the Mediterranean Countries 1450–1550: Some Historical Observations, *Oriental Carpet and*

Textile Studies II: Carpets of the Mediterranean Countries 1400–1600, pp. 13–28. Edited by Robert Pinner and Walter B. Denny. Hali OCTS Ltd., London.

Ryder, Michael, 1983, *Sheep and Man*. Duckworth, London.

1987a, Note on the Wool Type in Carpet Yarns from Pazyryk, *Oriental Carpet and Textile Studies III*, part 1, pp. 20–21. Edited by Robert Pinner and Walter B. Denny. Hali OCTS Ltd. and Hali Publications Ltd., London.

1987b, Wool Types, *Hali*, issue 34, May–June, p. 10. Hali Publications Ltd., London.

Sassouni, Viken, 1981, Armenian Church Floor Plan, *Hali*, vol. IV, no. 1, p. 24. Hali Publications Ltd., London.

Saunders, Peter E. (editor), 1981, *Tribal Visions: Catalogue of an Exhibition of Village and Nomad Carpets from Marin County Private Collections at Indian Valley Colleges from December 18, 1980 to January 12, 1981*. Marin Cultural Center, Novato.

Séguy, Marie-Rose, 1977, *The Miraculous Journey of Mahomet*. Translated from the French by Richard Pevear. G. Braziller, New York.

Sotheby's New York, 1993, *Turkmen and Antique Carpets from the Collection of Dr. and Mrs. Jon Thompson*. 16 December, no. 80. Sotheby's, New York.

Spuhler, Friedrich, 1986, "Chessboard" Rugs, *Oriental Carpet and Textile Studies II: Carpets of the Mediterranean Countries 1400–1600*, pp. 261–270. Edited by Robert Pinner and Walter B. Denny. Hali OCTS Ltd., London.

1987, *Die Orientteppiche im Museum für Islamische Kunst Berlin*. Staatliche Musees Preussischer Kulturbesitz, Berlin.

1988, Islamic Carpets and Textiles, *Islamic Art in the Keir Collection*, pp. 49–106. ABAS Foundation, London.

1998, *The Thyssen-Bornemisza Collection: Carpets and Textiles*. Translated by Maria Schlatter. Philip Wilson, London.

Sümer, Faruk, 1992, *Oğuzlar (Türkmenler): Tarihleri—Boy Teşkilatı—Destanları*. Türk Dünyası Araştırmaları Vakfı, İstanbul.

Suriano, Carlo Maria, 2001, Oak Leaves and Arabesques: Ushak Large-medallion Carpets with Pseudo-Kufic Borders, *Hali*, issue 116, May–June, pp. 106–115. Hali Publications Ltd., London.

Tanavoli, Parviz, 1985, *Shahsavan: Iranian Rugs and Textiles*. Rizzoli, New York.

Thompson, Jon, 1980, Centralised Designs, *Von Konya bis Kokand*, pp. 7–28. Eberhart Herrmann, Munich.

Uzunçarşılı, İsmail Hakkı, 1969, *Anadolu Beylikleri ve Akkoyunlu Karakoyunlu Devletleri*. Türk Tarih Kurumu Basımevi, Ankara.

Végh, Gyula, and Károly Layer, 1977, *Turkish Rugs in Transylvania*. New edition by Marino and Clara Dall'Oglio. Originally published by Éditions Charles Massin, Paris, in 1925. Crosby Press, Dyfed.

Völker, Angela, 2001, *Die orientalischen Knüpfteppich im MAK*. Österreichischen Museums für angewandte Kunst and Böhlau, Vienna, Cologne, and Weimar.

Vryonis, Speros, Jr., 1971, *The Decline of Medieval Hellenism in Asia Minor and the Process of Islamization from the Eleventh through the Fifteenth Century*. University of California Press, Berkeley, Los Angeles, and London.

Walker, Daniel S., 1982, *Oriental Rugs of the Hajji Babas*. Asia Society and H.N. Abrams in association with Sotheby's, New York.

Walker, John, 1979, *Old Master Paintings from the Collection of Baron Thyssen-Bornemisza*. International Exhibitions Foundation, Washington.

Woods, John E., 1999, *The Aqquyunlu: Clan, Confederation, Empire*. Revised and Expanded Edition. University of Utah Press, Salt Lake City.

Ydema, Onno, 1991, *Carpets and Their Datings in Netherlandish Paintings, 1540–1700*. Antique Collectors' Club Ltd., Woodbridge, Suffolk.

Yetkin, Şerare, 1981, *Historical Turkish Carpets*. Türkiye İş Bankası, İstanbul.

Index